1
38.45

364.36
Teen

TEEN RIGHTS AND FREEDOMS

| Juvenile Justice

TEEN RIGHTS AND FREEDOMS

I Juvenile Justice

David Haugen and Susan Musser
Book Editors

GREENHAVEN PRESS
A part of Gale, Cengage Learning

GALE
CENGAGE Learning·

Detroit • New York • San Francisco • New Haven, Conn • Waterville, Maine • London

Elizabeth Des Chenes, *Director, Publishing Solutions*

© 2013 Greenhaven Press, a part of Gale, Cengage Learning

Gale and Greenhaven Press are registered trademarks used herein under license.

For more information, contact:
Greenhaven Press
27500 Drake Rd.
Farmington Hills, MI 48331-3535
Or you can visit our Internet site at gale.cengage.com.

For product information and technology assistance, contact us at:

Gale Customer Support, 1-800-877-4253.
For permission to use material from this text or product, submit all requests online at www.cengage.com/permissions.

Further permissions questions can be emailed to permissionrequest@cengage.com.

Articles in Greenhaven Press anthologies are often edited for length to meet page requirements. In addition, original titles of these works are changed to clearly present the main thesis and to explicitly indicate the author's opinion. Every effort is made to ensure the Greenhaven Press accurately reflects the original intent of the authors. Every effort has been made to trace the owners of copyrighted material.

Cover Image: © Timothy Large/Shutterstock.com.

LIBRARY OF CONGRESS CATALOGING-IN-PUBLICATION DATA

Juvenile justice / David Haugen and Susan Musser, book editors.
    p. cm. -- (Teen rights and freedoms)
    Includes bibliographical references and index.
    ISBN 978-0-7377-6488-8 (hardcover)
1. Juvenile justice, Administration of--United States. 2. Teenagers--Legal status, laws, etc.--United States. I. Haugen, David M., 1969- II. Musser, Susan.
    KF9779.J883 2012
    364.360973--dc23

                                                                2012027814

Printed in the United States of America
1 2 3 4 5 6 7 17 16 15 14 13

Contents

incarcerated, he has grown to understand the crime's severity.

Foreword

> *"In the truest sense freedom cannot be
> bestowed, it must be achieved."*
> Franklin D. Roosevelt,
> September 16, 1936

The notion of children and teens having rights is a relatively recent development. Early in American history, the head of the household—nearly always the father—exercised complete control over the children in the family. Children were legally considered to be the property of their parents. Over time, this view changed, as society began to acknowledge that children have rights independent of their parents, and that the law should protect young people from exploitation. By the early twentieth century, more and more social reformers focused on the welfare of children, and over the ensuing decades advocates worked to protect them from harm in the workplace, to secure public education for all, and to guarantee fair treatment for youths in the criminal justice system. Throughout the twentieth century, rights for children and teens—and restrictions on those rights—were established by Congress and reinforced by the courts. Today's courts are still defining and clarifying the rights and freedoms of young people, sometimes expanding those rights and sometimes limiting them. Some teen rights are outside the scope of public law and remain in the realm of the family, while still others are determined by school policies.

Each volume in the Teen Rights and Freedoms series focuses on a different right or freedom and offers an anthology of key essays and articles on that right or freedom and the responsibilities that come with it. Material within each volume is drawn from a diverse selection of primary and secondary sources— journals, magazines, newspapers, nonfiction books, organization newsletters, position papers, speeches, and government documents, with a particular emphasis on Supreme Court and lower court decisions. Volumes also include first-person narratives from young people and others involved in teen rights issues, such as parents and educators. The material is selected and arranged to highlight all the major social and legal controversies relating to the right or freedom under discussion. Each selection is preceded by an introduction that provides context and background. In many cases, the essays point to the difference between adult and teen rights, and why this difference exists.

Many of the volumes cover rights guaranteed under the Bill of Rights and how these rights are interpreted and protected in regard to children and teens, including freedom of speech, freedom of the press, due process, and religious rights. The scope of the series also encompasses rights or freedoms, whether real or perceived, relating to the school environment, such as electronic devices, dress, Internet policies, and privacy. Some volumes focus on the home environment, including topics such as parental control and sexuality.

Numerous features are included in each volume of Teen Rights and Freedoms:

- An annotated **table of contents** provides a brief summary of each essay in the volume and highlights court decisions and personal narratives.

- An **introduction** specific to the volume topic gives context for the right or freedom and its impact on daily life.

- A brief **chronology** offers important dates associated with the right or freedom, including landmark court cases.

- **Primary sources**—including personal narratives and court decisions—are among the varied selections in the anthology.

- **Illustrations**—including photographs, charts, graphs, tables, statistics, and maps—are closely tied to the text and chosen to help readers understand key points or concepts.

- An annotated list of **organizations to contact** presents sources of additional information on the topic.
- A **for further reading** section offers a bibliography of books, periodical articles, and Internet sources for further research.
- A comprehensive subject **index** provides access to key people, places, events, and subjects cited in the text.

Each volume of Teen Rights and Freedoms delves deeply into the issues most relevant to the lives of teens: their own rights, freedoms, and responsibilities. With the help of this series, students and other readers can explore from many angles the evolution and current expression of rights both historic and contemporary.

Introduction

The concept of juvenile justice in the United States became solidified in the 1800s when social activists began advocating that young criminals were less blameworthy than adults for their crimes and more likely to be rehabilitated. In the early part of the nineteenth century, various reformers established schools to pull troubled youth off the streets. Part of the mission of these juvenile delinquency facilities was to provide youth with their own space away from the corrupting influences of the adult criminal system. In 1899, the first juvenile court in the United States appeared in Cook County, Illinois; its purpose, like the juvenile reformatories, was to separate wayward youth from adult criminals and focus sentencing on rehabilitation rather than jail time.

Julian Mack, one of the first judges to preside over the Cook County court, wrote in the 1909 *Harvard Law Review*:

> The child who must be brought into court should, of course, be made to know that he is face to face with the power of the state, but he should at the same time, and more emphatically, be made to feel that he is the object of its care and solicitude.

Judge Mack's comment reflects the notion of *parens patriae*, the guiding doctrine of juvenile justice. Latin for "parent of the country," *parens patriae* regards the juvenile offender as a person who is incapable of fully understanding the ramifications of crime and therefore requires the state to act as a guardian.

One tacit assumption of *parens patriae* is that the state understands what is best for the young offender and will act accordingly. That assumption, however, has been tested in the courts since the 1960s. The 1967 US Supreme Court case *In re Gault* involved Gerald Gault, a fifteen-year-old Arizona boy accused of making an indecent phone call to a neighbor. Arizona authorities removed Gault from his home without his parent's knowledge, and a judge passed sentence without sworn testimony of witnesses or the presence of legal counsel. The court ruled in Gault's favor and mandated that while the juvenile justice system may be separate, it must afford defendants with the protections of due process as defined by the Fourteenth Amendment.

Although *In re Gault* supported the enforcement of due process within juvenile courts, some observers believed this subverted the unique nature of juvenile justice. In 1971, the Supreme Court ruled in *McKeiver v. Pennsylvania* that unlike adults, juveniles are not entitled to a trial by jury. Supreme Court Justice Byron White argued that the juvenile justice system should not seek the same ends as adult criminal courts. Claiming that jury trials are no more a guarantee against excessive or punitive verdicts than a "conscientious judge" overseeing a juvenile case, White insisted that "a system eschewing blameworthiness and punishment for evil choice is itself an operative force against prejudice and short-tempered justice."

In the years since the *McKeiver* ruling, the differences between adult and juvenile proceedings have become less distinct. In a 2004 article for Washington University's *Journal of Gender, Social Policy and the Law*, Sandra M. Ko writes:

> The current juvenile justice system differs significantly from the juvenile justice system in place when the Court decided *McKeiver*. The current system incorporates many aspects of the adult criminal system. Many states now seek to punish children for their crimes and hold them accountable for their criminal conduct. This shift away from rehabilitation makes the policy arguments supporting *McKeiver* untenable.

Various issues remain contentious within the juvenile justice system. While some believe the juvenile system has incorporated too many facets of the adult criminal system, others contend that juveniles are not punished harshly enough. *Teen Rights and Freedoms: Juvenile Justice* examines the evolution of the juvenile justice system in the United States and its role in protecting youth and society at large.

Chronology

1825   In response to concern about the overcrowding of jails and corruption of youth imprisoned with adults, the first House of Refuge opens in New York to house juvenile criminal offenders, impoverished youth, and orphans.

1847   As Houses of Refuge are exposed for overcrowding, poor living conditions, and brutality, the first training school for boys is established in Massachusetts with an emphasis on schooling and vocational training for its residents.

1899   Cook County, Illinois, creates the first juvenile court, arguing that under the *parens patriae* doctrine the state can guide juvenile delinquents through rehabilitation.

1966   The US Supreme Court rules in *Kent v. United States* that juvenile offenders' due process rights must be observed in any court proceedings.

1967   The Supreme Court finds in *In re Gault* that any juvenile accused of a crime must be given the same due process rights as an adult during the delinquency proceeding.

1968   With the passage of the Juvenile Delinquency Prevention and Control Act, Congress promotes programs that fight juvenile delinquency on a local level.

1970   The Supreme Court holds in *In re Winship* that a court must prove a juvenile's crime beyond a reasonable doubt.

1971   The Supreme Court rules in *McKeiver v. Pennsylvania* that neither the Sixth nor Fourteenth Amendments guarantee juveniles the right to a trial by jury.

1974   The Juvenile Justice and Delinquency Prevention Act provides funds to states that enact programs emphasizing deinstitutionalization and separate adult and youth offenders.

1980   The jail removal provision of the Juvenile Justice and Delinquency Prevention Act of 1974 prohibits youth from being placed in adult facilities except in specific cases.

1989   The Supreme Court finds in *Stanford v. Kentucky* that any individual who is at least sixteen years of age when he or she commits a crime may be sentenced to death.

1992   The Disproportionate Minority Confinement clause is added to the Juvenile Justice and Delinquency Prevention Act of 1974 and calls on states to address the large number of minority youth in the juvenile justice system.

2005   In *Roper v. Simmons* the Supreme Court rules that it is unconstitutional to sentence juveniles under the age of eighteen to death; this overrules the previous decision which sanctioned the death penalty for any individual sixteen or older.

2010   In *Graham v. Florida* the Supreme Court finds it unconstitutional to sentence a juvenile offender to life without parole for any offense less than homicide.

> "Despite broad support within the academic, legal, and social-work professions, the [juvenile justice] ideal often failed to live up to its promise."

Reforming Juvenile Justice

Barry Krisberg

In the following viewpoint, a researcher details the ongoing evolution of juvenile rights and justice reform in the United States. He identifies the US Supreme Court decision of In re Gault *(1967) as the starting point of real change. This decision, coupled with the efforts of strong-minded reformers, led to the deinstitutionalization of juvenile offenders nationwide, according to the author. However, as crime rose in the 1980s and 1990s, legislators rescinded much of the earlier reform that had increased juvenile offenders' rights. Reformers pushed back, and the author credits these activists for a new round of deinstitutionalization that helped create the current juvenile justice system. Barry Krisberg is the director of research and policy and lecturer in residence at the Chief Justice Earl Warren Institute on Law and Social Policy at the University of California, Berkeley.*

In 1899, Illinois and Colorado established a new "Children's Court." The idea was to substitute treatment and care for punishment of delinquent youths. These changes were promoted

Barry Krisberg, "Reforming Juvenile Justice," *American Prospect*, vol. 16, no. 9, September 2005, pp. A2–A5. Copyright © 2005 by the American Prospect. All rights reserved. Reproduced by permission.

by child advocates such as the famous social activist Jane Addams and crusading judges like Denver's Ben Lindsey, as well as influential women's organizations and bar associations. Over the next 20 years, the concept of a separate court system for minors spread to most states. Although the new children's court movement lacked adequate resources to fulfill its lofty mission, the intellectual promise was virtually unchallenged for two-thirds of the 20th century.

Several key assumptions lay behind the juvenile-court idea. First, children were not just "small adults," and they needed to be handled differently. Second, there was a need for specially trained legal and correctional professionals to work with minors. Third, placing children in adult prisons and jails made them more antisocial and criminal. And finally, the emerging science of rehabilitation could rescue many of these troubled young people from lives of crime. In the intervening years, a wealth of research has validated each of these premises.

Despite broad support within the academic, legal, and social-work professions, the ideal often failed to live up to its promise. Over time, the juvenile-justice system in many states reverted to the punitive approach it was designed to replace. Though they were often called "training schools," the institutions were juvenile prisons. And the premise that the court, by definition, was acting "in the best interest of the child" left young offenders without the rights guaranteed to adult criminal defendants. There were repeated accounts of abusive practices. The duration of confinement was often unrelated to the severity of the offense. Juvenile hearings were usually secret, with no written transcripts and no right to appeal. Minors were not provided legal counsel, there were no safeguards against self-incrimination, and offenders were denied liberty without the due process of law guaranteed by the U.S. Constitution.

A series of legal challenges culminated in the landmark 1967 Supreme Court decision *In re Gault*. Writing for the Court, Justice Abe Fortas proclaimed, "Under our Constitution, the condition of being a boy does not justify a kangaroo court." Reviewing the case of 15-year-old Gerald Gault, who was sentenced to six years in an Arizona youth correctional facility for making an obscene phone call, the Court decreed that minors be afforded most of the due-process rights required in adult criminal courts.

Gault signaled a new era of reforms. One was a movement to divert as many youths as possible from the formal court system and to decriminalize "juvenile status offenses" such as truancy, running away, curfew violations, and incorrigibility. The 1970s witnessed widespread efforts to deinstitutionalize or "decarcerate" youngsters, moving them from secure detention centers and training schools to community-based programs that emphasized education and rehabilitation.

The most dramatic example came in 1972 in Massachusetts, where a respected reformer closed all of the state juvenile facilities and started over. Jerome Miller had been recruited to the state Department of Youth Services (DYS) to clean up a range of scandals and abuses. He encountered an intransigent bureaucracy. Corrections officers opposed even such modest reforms as letting youngsters wear street clothing instead of prison uniforms, or not requiring that their heads be completely shaven. Undeterred, Miller decided to close down the state's network of jail-like training schools. As the young inmates of the notorious Lyman School were loaded onto a bus that would take them to dorms at the University of Massachusetts, to be housed temporarily until being reassigned to community programs, one top Miller deputy proclaimed to the shocked guards, "You can have the institutions; we are taking the kids."

The training schools were replaced with a diverse network of small residential programs, typically with 25 children or fewer, located closer to the youths' home communities. A range of nonresidential programs included day reporting centers and intensive home-based supervision. The DYS continued to operate about half of the most secure facilities. Private nonprofits were recruited to run the rest, as well as all of the community-based programs.

A boy is accompanied into a Children's Court by a member of the Big Brothers organization in 1955. Children's Courts such as this one were first established in 1899 in Illinois and Colorado. © Orlando/Hulton Archive/Getty Images.

Although Miller left Massachusetts soon after becoming the department's youth-services commissioner, the Bay State continued to expand and refine the alternatives to the old prison-like training schools and never reopened the large juvenile institutions. Research by Harvard Law School and my organization, the National Council on Crime and Delinquency, showed that the Miller reforms successfully reduced the frequency and severity of new offenses of youth in the new programs compared with the training-school graduates.

As the Massachusetts model spread to many other states, Congress in 1974 created the federal Juvenile Justice and

Delinquency Prevention Act, with bipartisan backing. The act established a federal Office of Juvenile Justice and Delinquency Prevention (OJJDP) to conduct research, provide training, and make grants to states and jurisdictions that voluntarily complied with the act's mandates. The new law required participating states to remove status offenders and dependency cases from secure confinement, and to separate juveniles from adults by "sight and sound" in correctional facilities. In 1980, the act was amended to require that participating states remove minors from jails. Forty-eight states participated.

Miller went on to implement variations of his Massachusetts reforms in Pennsylvania and Illinois. Other states that broadly followed Miller's model included jurisdictions as politically diverse as Utah, Missouri, and Vermont. Often, publicity about abusive conditions in state facilities and lawsuits in federal courts catalyzed these reforms. From 1980 into the 1990s, Colorado, Indiana, Oklahoma, Maryland, Louisiana, Florida, Georgia, Rhode Island, and New Jersey were among states that began closing large, prison-like youth facilities. For a time, it appeared that the Miller reforms would become the "gold standard" for juvenile corrections, as the federal OJJDP provided training and support to jurisdictions seeking to replicate the Massachusetts approach.

The Invention of the "Super-Predator"

The rejection in some quarters of a reform model reflects both ideological preconceptions and misinformation about juvenile crime. Rates of serious violent juvenile crime as measured by the National Crime Survey were relatively constant between 1973 and 1989, then briefly rose by more than one-third and peaked in 1993. Some cited demographics, as the children of the baby boomers reached their teenage years. Others pointed to an epidemic of crack cocaine that fueled urban violence, as well as high unemployment and declining economic prospects for low-skilled workers, especially among minority groups. No one really knows for sure. But fear of a violent juvenile crime wave led some to predict a new cohort of "super-predators." Conservative academics such as James Q. Wilson and John Dilulio and a small band of mainstream criminologists such as Alfred Blumstein and James Fox forecast societal disaster. Wilson predicted "30,000 more young muggers, killers, and thieves;" Dilulio in 1990 foresaw another 270,000 violent juveniles by 2010. He warned of a "crime bomb" created by a generation of "fatherless, godless, and jobless [juvenile] super-predators."

The media hyped the story, and many elected officials exploited it. The citizenry was told about a generation of babies, born to "crack-addicted" mothers, who would possess permanent neurological damage, including the inability to feel empathy. The scientific evidence supporting this claim was nonexistent. More than 40 states made it easier to transfer children to adult criminal courts. Educators enacted "zero-tolerance" policies to make it easier to expel youngsters from school, and numerous communities adopted youth curfews. Many jurisdictions turned to metal detectors in public schools, random locker searches, drug tests for athletes, and mandatory school uniforms.

The panic was bipartisan. Every crime bill debated by Congress during the Clinton administration included new federal laws against juvenile crime. Paradoxically, as Attorney General Janet Reno advocated for wider and stronger social safety nets for vulnerable families, President Bill Clinton joined congressional leaders demanding tougher treatment of juvenile felons, including more incarceration in both the adult and youth correctional systems.

However, the much-advertised generation of super-predators never materialized. After 1993, rates of serious juvenile crime began a decade-long decline to historically low levels. And this juvenile-crime drop happened before the tougher juvenile penalties were even implemented. The fear-mongering social scientists had based their dire predictions on grossly inaccurate data and faulty reasoning, but the creators of the super-predator myth prevailed in the public-policy arena throughout most of the '90s.

As we approached the centennial of the American juvenile court, it looked like the juvenile-justice ideal was dying.

The Ideal of Juvenile Justice Survives

Despite adverse political currents, the juvenile-justice ideal has received a new lease on life thanks to pioneering efforts by states and by foundations, as well as the continuing programmatic influence of the federal approach begun in the 1970s and expanded during the Clinton-Reno era.

One key initiative of the federal OJJDP is known as Balanced and Restorative Justice. This approach, now embraced by many jurisdictions, places a major value on involving victims in the rehabilitative process. By coming to terms with harm done to victims, the youthful offender is also offered a way to restore his or her role in the community.

The second significant federal program is the Justice Department's Comprehensive Strategy for Serious, Violent, and Chronic Juvenile Offenders, first adopted in 1993. The research showed that a very small number of offenders committed most serious juvenile crimes, and that identification and control of these "dangerous few" was key. However, unlike the response to the supposed super-predators, this strategy does not call for an across-the-board crackdown on at-risk youth. A comprehensive body of research assembled by two senior Justice Department juvenile-justice officials, John J. Wilson and James C. Howell, showed that prevention was the most cost-effective response to youth crime, and that strengthening the family and other core institutions was the most important goal for a youth-crime-control strategy.

The proposed comprehensive strategy was adopted by Reno as the official policy position of the Justice Department in all matters relating to juvenile crime, and the program was successfully implemented in more than 50 communities nationwide. The basic idea was to help local leaders build their youth-service systems to provide "the right service, for the right youth, at the right time." This collaborative planning process helped policy-makers and professionals to debunk the myths about juvenile crime and to learn about interventions that were proven, as well as to foster more cooperative activities among multiple agencies. Most important, the effort showed community participants how to effectively respond to juvenile lawbreaking without resorting to mass-incarceration policies.

A third major national reform movement was launched by the Annie E. Casey Foundation in 1992. The goal: to reduce the overuse of juvenile-detention facilities and to redirect funding toward more effective services for at-risk youngsters. The foundation also sought to improve the conditions of confinement for detained youth and to reduce the overrepresentation of minority youths in detention.

The Casey Foundation approach required a multiagency planning process and included the development of improved risk screening, expansion of options for most detained youths, and efforts to expedite the processing of cases. After initial demonstration projects, the foundation has expanded the program to scores of communities. It also offers technical assistance and convenes an annual meeting. At the last such convening, in San Francisco, more than 700 people from across the nation gathered to discuss ways to further reduce unnecessary juvenile detention. The original demonstration project has led to a vibrant national movement, which includes high-quality replication manuals and a documentary, plus academic and professional publications.

These approaches all require collaborations among many sectors of the community. They all employ data and evidence-based practices to guide the reform agenda. Diversity is recognized as vital because one-size-fits-all programs usually fail. Instead, they seek to create a comprehensive continuum of appropriate services. Preventive strategies and early interventions are viewed as far more cost-effective than punitive approaches. All these programs place a great emphasis on involving youth, plus their families and neighbors, in shaping solutions. The core values of the juvenile-justice ideal continue to live. Like the reform im-

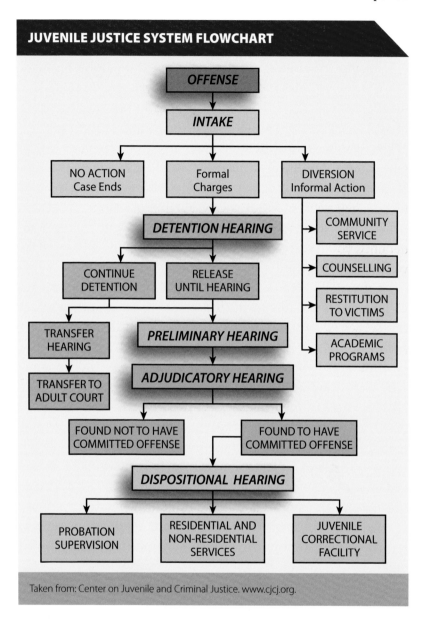

JUVENILE JUSTICE SYSTEM FLOWCHART

Taken from: Center on Juvenile and Criminal Justice. www.cjcj.org.

pulse of a century ago, the goal is to commit the juvenile-justice system to pursuing the best interests of the child, to strengthening family and community solutions to youth misconduct, and to emphasizing humane and fair treatment of the young.

In spite of the promise embodied in approaches like these, unlawful and brutal practices continue to plague youth correctional facilities in many states. Some jurisdictions are being investigated by the federal government for statutory and constitutional violations of the rights of institutionalized minors. In other locales, advocates for young people are successfully litigating against youth detention and corrections facilities. At the same time, the political hysteria surrounding the super-predator myth appears to be in remission. The chorus is growing to reject approaches such as youth correctional boot camps or "scared straight" programs that use prison visits to try to frighten youngsters away from criminal lives. While some of these dangerous programs continue to exist, many jurisdictions have shut them down. There is growing awareness about the prevalence of mental illness among institutionalized youngsters and the emergence of several initiatives to better meet their health-care needs.

This year's most positive development was the Supreme Court's decision to end the death penalty for those younger than 18 at the time of their offense. But this progress does not minimize the severe problems of the juvenile-justice system. Funding for services for troubled young people in the juvenile-justice and child-welfare systems remains woefully inadequate. Young people still do not have anything resembling adequate legal representation. Too many continue to be banished to the criminal-court system and languish in adult prisons. And racism, sexism, and class biases continue to tarnish the promise of equal justice for all.

The Way Forward

This *American Prospect* special supplement includes reports from places as diverse as California, Texas, New Mexico, Missouri, and Louisiana. All suggest that reform coalitions, often with strange bedfellows, can acknowledge the superiority of the reform approach and change practices that dehumanize young people and fail to reduce juvenile crime. By now the evidence is clear: Small, community-based approaches that stress prevention, education, and restitution rather than prison-like punishment are simply better policy. At the same time, as Ellis Cose recounts, racial disparities remain immense. And as Sam Rosenfeld reports, far too many children who need mental-health services are being dumped into the juvenile-justice system.

Given the overwhelming evidence that reform works, why is there continuing resistance? The answer to this question is complex. First and foremost, since the mid-'60s, crime policy in the United States has been heavily politicized. Democrats and Republicans have competed to position themselves as tough on crime. Being perceived as soft on juvenile offenders is considered a political liability. Second, the media continue to exaggerate the amount of violent crime committed by minors. Isolated stories about vicious crimes that are committed by very young adolescents are widely disseminated and become the grist for talk radio and other media commentary. The simplistic solution has been that tough responses to juvenile crime will deter youthful offenders.

Resistance to proven juvenile-justice models often comes from public-employee unions that fear the loss of jobs as traditional youth correctional facilities are downsized and some funding goes to community-based organizations. Also, severe state and local budget problems have led to a retrenchment in needed services, even as more innovative juvenile-justice models could actually save money. In some locales, organizations purporting to represent families of crime victims have lobbied for tougher penalties for juvenile offenders.

Progressive reforms are often undercut by entrenched biases about the predominantly poor and minority families caught up in the juvenile-justice system. These racial, ethnic, and class prejudices are too often reinforced by media reports that breed fear among the electorate about the "barbarians at the gates." As long as economic and fiscal pressures fuel anxiety over immigrants, the increased competition for jobs, and the deteriorating public-school system, it will be hard to generate compassionate and rational responses for youthful lawbreakers.

Jerome Miller once observed that the history of juvenile justice reflects a pattern of abuse and scandal followed by humanistic changes, but then a return to the previous conditions and bad practices. In a new millennium, one can only hope that proponents of the juvenile-justice ideal can figure out how to end this tragic cycle.

> "So wide a gulf between the State's
> treatment of the adult and of the child
> requires a bridge sturdier than mere
> verbiage, and reasons more persuasive
> than cliché can provide."

Juvenile Offenders Must Be Granted Due Process Rights Under the Fourteenth Amendment

The Supreme Court's Decision

Abe Fortas

In the following viewpoint, a US Supreme Court justice argues that while the juvenile justice system contains provisions that make it unique in comparison with the adult justice system, it cannot ignore the rights afforded all US citizens. In the 1967 ruling of In re Gault, *he states that age should not lead the courts to wield unlimited power over juveniles. This landmark decision ensured that juveniles would be afforded due process rights when charged with offenses within the juvenile justice system. Abe Fortas was an associate justice of the Supreme Court from 1965 to 1969.*

Abe Fortas, Opinion of the Court, *In re Gault*, US Supreme Court, May 15, 1967.

This is an appeal under 28 U.S.C. § 1257 from a judgment of the Supreme Court of Arizona affirming the dismissal of a petition for a writ of habeas corpus. The petition sought the release of Gerald Francis Gault, appellants' 15-year-old son, who had been committed as a juvenile delinquent to the State Industrial School by the Juvenile Court of Gila County, Arizona. The Supreme Court of Arizona affirmed dismissal of the writ against various arguments which included an attack upon the constitutionality of the Arizona Juvenile Code because of its alleged denial of procedural due process rights to juveniles charged with being "delinquents." The court agreed that the constitutional guarantee of due process of law is applicable in such proceedings. It held that Arizona's Juvenile Code is to be read as "impliedly" implementing the "due process concept." It then proceeded to identify and describe "the particular elements which constitute due process in a juvenile hearing." It concluded that the proceedings ending in commitment of Gerald Gault did not offend those requirements. We do not agree, and we reverse. . . .

The Bill of Rights Is Not Only for Adults

The Supreme Court of Arizona held that due process of law is requisite to the constitutional validity of proceedings in which a court reaches the conclusion that a juvenile has been at fault, has engaged in conduct prohibited by law, or has otherwise misbehaved, with the consequence that he is committed to an institution in which his freedom is curtailed. This conclusion is in accord with the decisions of a number of courts under both federal and state constitutions.

This Court has not heretofore decided the precise question. In *Kent v. United States*, (1966), we considered the requirements for a valid waiver of the "exclusive" jurisdiction of the Juvenile Court of the District of Columbia so that a juvenile could be tried in the adult criminal court of the District. Although our decision turned upon the language of the statute, we emphasized the necessity that "the basic requirements of due process and fairness" be satisfied in such proceedings. *Haley v. Ohio*, (1948), involved the admissibility, in a state criminal court of general jurisdiction, of a confession by a 15-year-old boy. The Court held that the Fourteenth Amendment applied to prohibit the use of the coerced confession. Mr. Justice [William O.] Douglas said, "Neither man nor child can be allowed to stand condemned by methods which flout constitutional requirements of due process of law." To the same effect is *Gallegos v. Colorado* (1962). Accordingly, while these cases relate only to restricted aspects of the subject, they unmistakably indicate that, whatever may be their precise impact, neither the Fourteenth Amendment nor the Bill of Rights is for adults alone.

We do not in this opinion consider the impact of these constitutional provisions upon the totality of the relationship of the juvenile and the state. We do not even consider the entire process relating to juvenile "delinquents." For example, we are not here concerned with the procedures or constitutional rights applicable to the pre-judicial stages of the juvenile process, nor do we direct our attention to the post-adjudicative or dispositional process. We consider only the problems presented to us by this case. These relate to the proceedings by which a determination is made as to whether a juvenile is a "delinquent" as a result of alleged misconduct on his part, with the consequence that he may be committed to a state institution. As to these proceedings, there appears to be little current dissent from the proposition that the Due Process Clause has a role to play. The problem is to ascertain the precise impact of the due process requirement upon such proceedings.

Due Process Is Necessary for Justice

From the inception of the juvenile court system, wide differences have been tolerated—indeed insisted upon—between the procedural rights accorded to adults and those of juveniles. In practically all jurisdictions, there are rights granted to adults which are withheld from juveniles. In addition to the specific problems involved in the present case, for example, it has been held that the juvenile is not entitled to bail, to indictment by grand jury, to a public trial or to trial by jury. It is frequent practice that rules governing the arrest and interrogation of adults by the police are not observed in the case of juveniles. . . .

The highest motives and most enlightened impulses led to a peculiar system for juveniles, unknown to our law in any comparable context. The constitutional and theoretical basis for this peculiar system is—to say the least—debatable. And in practice, as we remarked in the *Kent* case, the results have not been entirely satisfactory. Juvenile Court history has again demonstrated that unbridled discretion, however benevolently motivated, is frequently a poor substitute for principle and procedure. . . . The absence of substantive standards has not necessarily meant that children receive careful, compassionate, individualized treatment. The absence of procedural rules based upon constitutional principle has not always produced fair, efficient, and effective procedures. Departures from established principles of due process have frequently resulted not in enlightened procedure, but in arbitrariness. The Chairman of the Pennsylvania Council of Juvenile Court Judges has recently observed:

> Unfortunately, loose procedures, high-handed methods and crowded court calendars, either singly or in combination, all too often, have resulted in depriving some juveniles of fundamental rights that have resulted in a denial of due process.

Failure to observe the fundamental requirements of due process has resulted in instances, which might have been avoided, of unfairness to individuals and inadequate or inaccurate findings of fact and unfortunate prescriptions of remedy. Due process of law is the primary and indispensable foundation of individual freedom. It is the basic and essential term in the social compact which defines the rights of the individual and delimits

The Justification for Individual Justice Within Juvenile Courts

Juvenile courts stress individuation almost to the exclusion of justice. Individuation means that treatment depends on what a person is, not on what he has done. Juvenile statutes typically define as delinquent a child who has done no more than violate a municipal ordinance; hence, almost any child may be subject to juvenile court jurisdiction. Society fines an adult who disobeys a littering ordinance but may treat a juvenile who violates the same ordinance in exactly the same way it treats a juvenile who commits murder.

The legal justification for individual justice is found in the doctrine of *parens patriae*: Towards its wayward children the state acts not as governor but as parent. Because a child who engages in delinquent conduct needs care, the state, as a loving parent, intervenes to care for him. It is obviously in the child's best interest that the state care for him and cure him of the problems which resulted in his delinquency. Therefore, procedural formality should not block a finding of delinquency. . . . A finding of delinquency brings the child beneficial, rather than harmful, results.

Janet Friedman Stansby, "In re Gault: Children Are People," California Law Review, *October 1967.*

the powers which the state may exercise. As Mr. Justice [Felix] Frankfurter has said: "The history of American freedom is, in no small measure, the history of procedure." But, in addition, the procedural rules which have been fashioned from the generality of due process are our best instruments for the distillation and evaluation of essential facts from the conflicting welter of data that life and our adversary methods present. It is these instruments of due process which enhance the possibility that truth will emerge from the confrontation of opposing versions and conflicting data. "Procedure is to law what 'scientific method' is to science." . . .

Due Process Gives Court Decisions Validity

Further, it is urged that the juvenile benefits from informal proceedings in the court. The early conception of the Juvenile Court proceeding was one in which a fatherly judge touched the heart and conscience of the erring youth by talking over his problems, by paternal advice and admonition, and in which, in extreme situations, benevolent and wise institutions of the State provided guidance and help "to save him from a downward career." Then, as now, goodwill and compassion were admirably prevalent. But recent studies have, with surprising unanimity, entered sharp dissent as to the validity of this gentle conception. They suggest that the appearance as well as the actuality of fairness, impartiality and orderliness—in short, the essentials of due process—may be a more impressive and more therapeutic attitude so far as the juvenile is concerned. For example, in a recent study, the sociologists [Stanton] Wheeler and [Leonard S.] Cottrell observe that, when the procedural laxness of the "*parens patriae*" [the state as parent] attitude is followed by stern disciplining, the contrast may have an adverse effect upon the child, who feels that he has been deceived or enticed. They conclude as follows:

> Unless appropriate due process of law is followed, even the juvenile who has violated the law may not feel that he is being fairly treated, and may therefore resist the rehabilitative efforts of court personnel.

Of course it is not suggested that juvenile court judges should fail appropriately to take account, in their demeanor and conduct, of the emotional and psychological attitude of the juveniles with whom they are confronted. While due process requirements will, in some instances, introduce a degree of order and regularity to Juvenile Court proceedings to determine delinquency, and in contested cases will introduce some elements of the adversary system, nothing will require that the conception of the kindly juvenile judge be replaced by its opposite, nor do we here rule upon the question whether ordinary due process requirements must be observed with respect to hearings to determine the disposition of the delinquent child.

The Circumstances of Each Case Must Be Considered

Ultimately, however, we confront the reality of that portion of the Juvenile Court process with which we deal in this case. A boy is charged with misconduct. The boy is committed to an institution where he may be restrained of liberty for years. It is of no constitutional consequence—and of limited practical meaning—that the institution to which he is committed is called an Industrial School. The fact of the matter is that, however euphemistic the title, a "receiving home" or an "industrial school" for juveniles is an institution of confinement in which the child is incarcerated for a greater or lesser time. . . . Instead of mother and father and sisters and brothers and friends and classmates, his world is peopled by guards, custodians, state employees, and "delinquents" confined with him for anything from waywardness to rape and homicide.

In view of this, it would be extraordinary if our Constitution did not require the procedural regularity and the exercise of care implied in the phrase "due process." Under our Constitution, the condition of being a boy does not justify a kangaroo court. The traditional ideas of Juvenile Court procedure, indeed, contemplated that time would be available and care would be used to establish precisely what the juvenile did and why he did it— was it a prank of adolescence or a brutal act threatening serious consequences to himself or society unless corrected? Under traditional notions, one would assume that, in a case like that of Gerald Gault, where the juvenile appears to have a home, a working mother and father, and an older brother, the Juvenile

Youths accused of burglaries shield their faces from photographers in a Queens, New York, police precinct in 1961. Juvenile offenders were granted due process rights by a landmark 1967 US Supreme Court decision. © Bettmann/Corbis.

Judge would have made a careful inquiry and judgment as to the possibility that the boy could be disciplined and dealt with at home, despite his previous transgressions. Indeed, so far as appears in the record before us, except for some conversation with Gerald about his school work and his "wanting to go to . . . Grand Canyon with his father," the points to which the judge directed his attention were little different from those that would be involved in determining any charge of violation of a penal statute. The essential difference between Gerald's case and a normal criminal case is that safeguards available to adults were discarded in Gerald's case. The summary procedure as well as the long commitment was possible because Gerald was 15 years of age instead of over 18.

The Wide Gap Between Juvenile and Adult Justice

If Gerald had been over 18, he would not have been subject to Juvenile Court proceedings. For the particular offense immediately involved, the maximum punishment would have been a fine of $5 to $50, or imprisonment in jail for not more than two months. Instead, he was committed to custody for a maximum of six years. If he had been over 18 and had committed an offense to which such a sentence might apply, he would have been entitled to substantial rights under the Constitution of the United States as well as under Arizona's laws and constitution. The United States Constitution would guarantee him rights and protections with respect to arrest, search and seizure, and pretrial interrogation. It would assure him of specific notice of the charges and adequate time to decide his course of action and to prepare his defense. He would be entitled to clear advice that he could be represented by counsel, and, at least if a felony were involved, the State would be required to provide counsel if his parents were unable to afford it. If the court acted on the basis of his confession, careful procedures would be required to assure its voluntariness. If the case went to trial, confrontation and opportunity for cross-examination would be guaranteed. So wide a gulf between the State's treatment of the adult and of the child requires a bridge sturdier than mere verbiage, and reasons more persuasive than cliché can provide. As Wheeler and Cottrell have put it:

> The rhetoric of the juvenile court movement has developed without any necessarily close correspondence to the realities of court and institutional routines.

Juveniles Must Be Treated Fairly

In *Kent v. United States*, we stated that the Juvenile Court Judge's exercise of the power of the state as *parens patriae* was not unlimited. We said that "the admonition to function in a 'parental' relationship is not an invitation to procedural arbitrariness." With respect to the waiver by the Juvenile Court to the adult court of jurisdiction over an offense committed by a youth, we said that:

> There is no place in our system of law for reaching a result of such tremendous consequences without ceremony—without hearing, without effective assistance of counsel, without a statement of reasons.

We announced with respect to such waiver proceedings that [:]

> We do not mean . . . to indicate that the hearing to be held must conform with all of the requirements of a criminal trial or even of the usual administrative hearing; but we do hold that the hearing must measure up to the essentials of due process and fair treatment.

We reiterate this view, here in connection with a juvenile court adjudication of "delinquency," as a requirement which is part of the Due Process Clause of the Fourteenth Amendment of our Constitution.

> "The absence of due process can lead to inaccurate outcomes in criminal proceedings, including false confessions and conviction of the innocent."

Juvenile Criminal Proceedings Should Restore Focus on Minors' Due Process Rights by Returning to Standards Set in *In re Gault*

Benjamin E. Friedman

In the following viewpoint, a lawyer maintains that the granting of due process rights to minors in In re Gault *was based on the importance of finding truth; however, subsequent rulings made it possible for juveniles to waive these rights, even if they did not fully understand the consequences of the waiver. Due to the incomplete psychological development of minors, the author calls for a return to a stricter adherence to the principles introduced in* Gault. *Benjamin E. Friedman is a litigation associate for the Los Angeles law firm Munger, Tolles and Olson LLP.*

The juvenile court system came into being over a century ago amidst a series of progressive reforms recognizing that

Benjamin E. Friedman, "Protecting the Truth: An Argument for Juvenile Rights and a Return to *In re Gault*," *UCLA Law Review Discourse*, vol. 58, 2011. Copyright © 2011 by Benjamin Friedman. All rights reserved. Reproduced by permisison.

children had different needs than adults. The new courts were based on a model of rehabilitation and care rather than punishment. Because the courts were viewed as helping juveniles instead of subjecting them to criminal penalties, judges dispensed with many of the constitutional rights and procedures inherent to adult criminal proceedings.

From its inception, the juvenile court was criticized for failing to live up to its ideal of providing therapeutic, individualized treatment to juvenile delinquents. Critics claimed the proceedings in practice were much closer to criminal proceedings, and juvenile judges abused their broad discretion. The U.S. Supreme Court addressed these concerns in the 1967 case *In re Gault*, which granted juveniles procedural rights in court proceedings, including the right to legal counsel and the privilege against self-incrimination.

Juvenile Waivers Increase Self-Incrimination

The courts could have read *Gault* broadly to require additional protections to juveniles greater than those granted to adults. But the Supreme Court has never mandated additional protections based on the age of a suspect. Instead, subsequent cases at best granted equivalent rights and at worst gave children lesser protections. In *Fare v. Michael C.* [1979], the Court held that the validity of a juvenile's waiver of his privilege against self-incrimination and of his right to counsel would be judged under the same flexible totality of the circumstances test applied to adults, with youth as merely one factor to consider.

While a totality test allows the possibility of enhanced protections because of youth, in practice judges tend not to weigh age heavily when determining whether the waiver of rights was valid (that is, knowing and voluntary). As a result, courts deem juvenile waivers valid the vast majority of the time, leaving children to negotiate police interactions without the aid of an attorney. This unsympathetic treatment of juveniles is likely due to a perceived increase in youth crime and violence, which has driven courts and legislatures to eschew the therapeutic model of juvenile courts in favor of a more punitive standard.

This retreat from *Gault* does not easily reconcile with increased research showing that children are fundamentally different from adults in comprehending and exercising their rights, and that it is almost impossible to judge whether a juvenile is competent to waive his constitutional protections. Further, *Michael C.* overlooked a key concern in *Gault*: The absence of due process can lead to inaccurate outcomes in criminal proceedings, including false confessions and conviction of the innocent. *Gault* was indeed prescient. In the four decades since that opinion, advances in investigatory techniques, including DNA technology, have shown that false confessions are a very real phenomenon of particular danger to juveniles vulnerable to the coercive environment of an interrogation room.

This [viewpoint] discusses the importance of a return to *Gault's* principles: providing juveniles enhanced due process protections to ensure the accuracy of legal proceedings and to prevent wrongful convictions based on false confessions. . . .

Protection of Dignity vs. Protection of Truth

Gault could be seen as somewhat analogous to *Miranda v. Arizona* [1966], decided by the Supreme Court a year earlier. *Miranda,* which involved adult defendants, held that a statement obtained from a suspect during custodial interrogation by police was admissible as evidence only if it had been preceded by admonitions informing the suspect of his constitutional rights and guarantees against self-incrimination. The police must tell the suspect that he has the right to remain silent, that any statement he makes could be used as evidence against him, and that he has the right to legal counsel, "either retained or appointed." Similarly, *Gault* affirmed a juvenile's right to legal counsel and privilege against self-incrimination.

The reasoning behind the two holdings, however, is strikingly different. *Miranda* was premised on procedural rights that prevent the police from compelling an individual to provide a confession against his will. The concern was the "respect a government . . . must accord to the dignity and integrity of its citizens." Procedural rights served to "respect the inviolability of the human personality" and to limit the "scope of governmental power over the citizen." A confession, even if truthful and corroborated by other evidence, would be inadmissible if not given voluntarily. In other words, the privilege against self-incrimination was of such importance that the Court would rather let a guilty man go free than allow police tactics that led to an involuntary confession or even a voluntary confession that was not preceded by the *Miranda* warnings.

Gault, in contrast, based its reasoning on the need for accuracy in the factfinding process rather than on protecting juveniles' dignity in court proceedings. The majority began its discussion of the privilege against self-incrimination with a quotation about the dangers of false confessions, stating "[t]he privilege against self-incrimination is, of course, related to the question of the safeguards necessary to assure that admissions or confessions are *reasonably trustworthy,* that they are not the mere fruits of fear or coercion, but are *reliable expressions of the truth.*" The opinion devoted several pages to the discussion of prior cases of juveniles giving false or unreliable confessions. The Court explicitly noted that in a past juvenile court ruling that excluded oral statements, "[the court] did not rest its decision on a showing that the statements were involuntary, but because they were untrustworthy." This was a clear contrast to *Miranda's* exclusion of trustworthy statements if they were obtained at the cost of a suspect's personal dignity. Whereas *Miranda* was primarily concerned that confessions be voluntary, *Gault* was concerned that confessions be trustworthy.

This concern for truth is understandable given that the juvenile court convicted Gault based on an unsubstantiated admission

Juveniles sometimes waive their rights when arrested because they do not fully understand them. Some legal scholars believe that closer adherence to the principles of due process set by In re Gault *would protect juveniles.* © Michael Crockett Photography/The Image Bank/ Getty Images.

of guilt, with no opportunity to cross examine the chief witness against him. Unlike *Miranda*, in which the Court was concerned with coerced but possibly true statements, the *Gault* Court was faced with a juvenile deprived of his liberty based on untrustworthy evidence.

Thus, in *Gault*, constitutional procedure served to protect the truth: "It is these instruments of due process which enhance the possibility that truth will emerge from the confrontation of opposing versions and conflicting data. 'Procedure is to law what "scientific method" is to science.'" Constitutional protections and procedures do not simply protect individuals from excessive government encroachment on their dignity but also protect the accuracy of factfinding.

Juvenile Rights After *In re Gault*

This theme of procedure as a guarantee of accuracy continued in subsequent juvenile cases. In *In re Winship* [1970], which held that charges against juveniles must be proved beyond a reasonable doubt, the Supreme Court stated that the reasonable doubt standard "is a prime instrument for reducing the risk of convictions based on factual error." However, the accuracy justification was also used to deny juveniles certain rights. In *McKeiver v. Pennsylvania* [1971], the Court denied juveniles the right to a jury trial on the basis that juries were not necessary for accurate factfinding.

Some scholars predicted that the *Gault* ruling would lead to expansive procedural protections for juveniles. *Gault* implied these broad protections when the Court suggested that in obtaining admissions of guilt from children, "the *greatest care* must be taken to assure that the admission . . . was not the product of ignorance of rights or of adolescent fantasy, fright, or despair." However, at best the Court went on to grant juveniles equivalent rights to adults, such as in *Winship*. And the Court was not even willing to grant juveniles all the protections of the criminal justice system, as evidenced by *McKeiver*'s denial of a right to a jury trial. So despite *Gault*'s admonition to take "the greatest care," juveniles were not granted any special protections in deference to their youth.

Fare v. Michael C. Further Erodes Juvenile Rights

Any vestige of hope that *Gault* would lead to greater protections for juveniles was derailed by *Fare v. Michael C.*, in which a more conservative Court held that a juvenile's waiver of his *Miranda* rights would be evaluated under the same totality of circumstances test applied to adult waivers. The police arrested Michael C., age sixteen and a half, on suspicion of murder. During police interrogation, he requested to see his probation officer. After the police denied his request, Michael C. gave several incriminating statements that resulted in his placement into juvenile proceedings. In ruling on a suppression motion, the California Supreme Court held that the request for a probation officer was equivalent to invoking the right to an attorney, which under *Miranda* would have required the police to cease their questioning.

The U.S. Supreme Court overturned the California Supreme Court in a 5-4 decision, stating that a probation officer did not serve the same function as an attorney, and therefore requesting one did not invoke the *Miranda* rule. As to whether Michael C., absent the request for the probation officer, had "knowingly and intelligently" waived his *Miranda* protections, the Court said the appropriate test was to evaluate the totality of circumstances, taking into account the juvenile's "age, experience, education, background, and intelligence." Since Michael C. had been informed of his rights, had prior experience with the police, and was of normal intelligence, the Court held that he had properly understood and waived his rights.

The *Michael C.* opinion, which did not cite *Gault* at all, gives no indication of concern that the defendant's incriminating statements might be untrustworthy. There is no mention of

Juveniles Have Difficulty Understanding Their Rights

Studies to evaluate the ability of juveniles to understand the *Miranda* warnings have produced conclusions similar to those offered by scientific research. In one study, eighty-six of ninety juveniles studied, waived their *Miranda* rights and confessed. The study dealt primarily with fourteen-year-olds and concluded that as a group, they were likely incapable of "knowingly and intelligently understanding their rights." Another study found that comprehension of *Miranda* warnings was tied to age, and that understanding did not increase with prior criminal experience. Although both of these tests found increasing comprehension after age fourteen, neither study evaluated older minors' ability to fully appreciate the consequences of waiving their rights. Together, these studies indicate that minors have a difficulty fully comprehending their rights; that prior experience does not have a significant impact on comprehension; and that minors confess more often than adults. A third study showed that minors under the age of sixteen are unable to fully understand their constitutional rights. In this study, four-fifths of the minors interviewed did not understand at least a portion of the *Miranda* warnings; the minors had special difficulty applying the right to remain silent. A majority of the minors thought that a court could compel their testimony. Of the minors studied, ninety percent waived their right to remain silent.

> Michael Wayne Brooks, *"Kids Waiving Goodbye to Their Rights: An Argument Against Juveniles' Ability to Waive Their Right to Remain Silent During Police Interrogations,"* George Mason Law Review, *Fall 2004.*

the possibility of a false confession. The Court was faced with an admitted murderer, and extending special protections based on his youth would have resulted in a murderer going free. The Court applied the standard *Miranda* rule, granting Michael C.

the same right of waiver and test of voluntariness that applied to adults. Age became just one of a long list of factors to be considered, and in this case the majority gave it no particular weight—in fact, when applying the totality test to the circumstances of the case, the Court did not discuss Michael C.'s age at all other than to mention that he was sixteen and a half. Thus, although *Michael C.* did not overturn *Gault*, it signaled an end to the hope that *Gault* would lead to special constitutional protections for juveniles.

Moving Away from the Best-Interests Model

Under *Gault*, juveniles have more procedural rights than previously granted in juvenile courts, yet these rights must be affirmatively invoked and may be waived as long as the waiver is knowing and voluntary under the *Michael C.* totality test. Theoretically, this test allows judges the discretion to weigh the age of a child more heavily and thereby extend greater protections to juveniles. In practice, however, judges generally do not grant these protections. [Associate Juvenile Court Justice] Kenneth King's analysis of several hundred juvenile-waiver cases reveals only "grudging, if any, accommodations to the youth of the accused." While some states have adopted rules rendering certain juvenile interrogations per se inadmissible if a parent or other interested adult is not present, thirty-five states and the District of Columbia use the *Michael C.* totality test without modification. Many state courts analyze waiver under adult *Miranda* jurisprudence, which takes no account of a suspect's age and therefore often leads to a finding of valid waiver. The legacy of *Michael C.* is that juveniles now are found to have validly waived their *Miranda* protections more than 90 percent of the time.

The application of the *Michael C.* test reflects a trend of states moving away from the rehabilitative best-interests model of the juvenile courts. States now emphasize punishment based on public safety concerns, and courts assert "society's [need for] self-preservation" as a justification for rejecting greater procedural protections for juveniles.

Moreover, states have instituted harsher penalties for juveniles, and all fifty states have recently passed laws permitting juveniles to be tried as adults. The lack of sympathy towards juveniles is likely a result of a perceived increase in youth crime, particularly violent crime, coupled with the seeming ineffectiveness of the rehabilitative ideal of the juvenile courts. Indeed, from the mid-eighties to the early nineties, the period following *Michael C.*, violent crime by juveniles increased 57 percent, and by 1992, one in seven homicide arrests was a juvenile. Some commentators have claimed that the media has played an important role in exaggerating the problem, causing a public perception that juvenile crime is out of control. Whatever the cause, the result is that in the years following *Gault* and *Michael C.*, society and the courts have come to view juveniles as a potential menace rather than as vulnerable and in need of special protections.

There Are Fundamental Differences Between Children and Adults

This unsympathetic view of juveniles is in tension with substantial empirical, psychological, and neurological research establishing that children are fundamentally different from adults when it comes to understanding and invoking their rights. In fact, [according to law professor Steven Drizin and law clerk Greg Luloff] "age and intelligence remain the primary predictors of *Miranda* comprehension." Research on juvenile brain development suggests that adolescents are "physiologically incapable" of thinking like adults. Capacity to reason is based on "brain development and growth" more than "intellectual development." The frontal cortex of the brain, which is used in making informed decisions, is the last part of the brain to develop and therefore is of decreased ability in juveniles.

Kenneth King finds that "[e]ven if an adolescent has an 'adult-like' capacity to make decisions, the adolescent's sense of time, lack of future orientation, labile emotions, calculus of risk and gain, and vulnerability to pressure will often drive him or her to make very different decisions than an adult would in similar circumstances." The difference becomes more apparent in situations of stress, such as police interrogations or court proceedings. Immaturity can produce the same lack of capacity as mental illness, which means that many juveniles are in fact legally incompetent. This is especially the case in the juvenile justice system, in which children generally have below-average intelligence and the majority have mental disorders.

Juveniles' conditioned behavior may also lead to the mistaken assumption that they have validly waived their rights. Children are raised to be obedient to adults, which makes them highly susceptible to coercion by authority figures, such as police, who may urge them to waive their rights. External showings of understanding by children, such as nodding or not asking questions—which a court may presume indicate valid waiver—may instead be a child's effort to please adults rather than to indicate true comprehension. Further, while the *Michael C.* totality test includes prior experience with law enforcement as a factor, studies have shown that previous involvement with police and the juvenile courts does not enhance understanding of one's rights.

Although some juveniles may be capable of validly waiving their rights, psychiatric experts have asserted that it is nearly impossible for clinicians to make accurate determinations of an individual juvenile's competence or capacity. This suggests that a juvenile-court judge or police officer would be equally incapable of assessing whether a juvenile is competent to waive his or her rights. Justice Marshall may have implied this in his *Michael C.* dissent when he said, "I do not believe a case-by-case approach [to waiver] provides police sufficient guidance, or affords juveniles adequate protection."

Age Is of Central Concern to the Waiver of Rights

The conclusion to be drawn from this evidence is that age is not simply one of many factors to be considered in determining the validity of a waiver—it is the central issue. If the concern in *Miranda* was protecting individuals' dignity in custodial interrogation from encroachment and coercion by government actors, such protection is not extended to children merely by giving them protections equivalent to adults. Juveniles cannot in many circumstances give a truly valid waiver. It is nearly impossible for psychiatric experts, much less police officers or judges, to distinguish valid waivers by juveniles from invalid ones.

Yet despite this strong evidence, courts and legislatures have been reluctant to extend special protections or accommodations based on age. This was evidenced by *Michael C.*, in which the Court found the waiver valid despite the defendant's age. Perhaps this unwillingness is an inevitable result of an environment both fearful of and hostile towards youth. The dignity arguments of *Miranda* and, by extension, of *Michael C.* are outweighed by concerns for public safety and effective law enforcement. . . .

The majority in *Gault*, was concerned that juveniles were getting "'the worst of both worlds,'" lacking both the full constitutional protections of adults and the specialized therapeutic attention promised by juvenile courts. Today, that concern remains mostly unaddressed. While children ostensibly have greater procedural rights than they did before *Gault*, the current application of the *Michael C.* totality test results in waiver of those rights over 90 percent of the time, effectively leaving juveniles without meaningful constitutional protections. At the same time, states have eschewed the rehabilitative ideal of juvenile courts, resulting in harsher treatment of minors suspected of crimes and a general unwillingness to extend any special protections to children beyond the pro forma [for the sake of formality] *Miranda* warnings.

Yet whatever one's position on the dangers of youth violence and the proper balance of public safety and individual rights, it is clear that wrongfully convicting the innocent advances no one's interest except that of the true perpetrator. Until recently, it could be said that the false confessions leading to wrongful convictions were only hypothetical. But as more research reveals the reality of false confessions, the need to return to *Gault*'s principles becomes more pressing. Juveniles need greater procedural protections, not to burden law enforcement and coddle criminals, but to ensure that when society applies its potent authority to strip individuals of their freedom, it does so accurately.

> "If the formalities of the criminal adjudicative process are to be superimposed upon the juvenile court system, there is little need for its separate existence."

Neither the Sixth nor Fourteenth Amendment Guarantees a Juvenile Offender the Right to a Trial by Jury

The Supreme Court's Decision

Harry Blackmun

In the following viewpoint, a US Supreme Court justice argues that jury trials are not guaranteed by the Sixth and Fourteenth Amendments within the juvenile justice system. The author contends that jury trials will corrupt the rehabilitative nature of the system and disrupt the ability of states to craft individualized legislation. He concludes that as long as there remains a separation between the criminal and juvenile systems, jury trials should be reserved only for adults. Harry Blackmun was an associate justice of the Supreme Court from 1970 to 1994.

Plurality opinion, *McKeiver v. Pennsylvania*, US Supreme Court, June 21, 1971.

The right to an impartial jury "[i]n all criminal prosecutions" under federal law is guaranteed by the Sixth Amendment. Through the Fourteenth Amendment, that requirement has now been imposed upon the States "in all criminal cases which—were they to be tried in a federal court—would come within the Sixth Amendment's guarantee." This is because the Court has said it believes "that trial by jury in criminal cases is fundamental to the American scheme of justice" [*Duncan v. Louisiana* (1968); *Bloom v. Illinois* (1968)].

This, of course, does not automatically provide the answer to the present jury trial issue, if for no other reason than that the juvenile court proceeding has not yet been held to be a "criminal prosecution" within the meaning and reach of the Sixth Amendment, and also has not yet been regarded as devoid of criminal aspects merely because it usually has been given the civil label.

Determining the Impact of Due Process in Juvenile Proceedings

Little, indeed, is to be gained by any attempt simplistically to call the juvenile court proceeding either "civil" or "criminal." The Court carefully has avoided this wooden approach. Before [*In re*] *Gault* was decided in 1967 [and found that juveniles' due process rights must be observed in the hearing process], the Fifth Amendment's guarantee against self-incrimination had been imposed upon the state criminal trial. So, too, had the Sixth Amendment's rights of confrontation and cross-examination. Yet the Court did not automatically and peremptorily apply those rights to the juvenile proceeding. A reading of *Gault* reveals the opposite. And the same separate approach to the standard of proof issue is evident from the carefully separated application of the standard, first to the criminal trial and then to the juvenile proceeding, displayed in [*In re*] *Winship* (1970).

Thus, accepting "the proposition that the Due Process Clause has a role to play," *Gault*, our task here with respect to trial by jury, as it was in *Gault* with respect to other claimed rights, "is to ascertain the precise impact of the due process requirement."

Juvenile Proceedings Are Substantially Similar to a Criminal Trial

The Pennsylvania juveniles' basic argument is that they were tried in proceedings "substantially similar to a criminal trial." They say that a delinquency proceeding in their State is initiated by a petition charging a penal code violation in the conclusory language of an indictment; that a juvenile detained prior to trial is held in a building substantially similar to an adult prison; that, in Philadelphia, juveniles over 16 are, in fact, held in the cells of a prison; that counsel and the prosecution engage in plea bargaining; that motions to suppress are routinely heard and decided; that the usual rules of evidence are applied; that the customary common law defenses are available; that the press is generally admitted in the Philadelphia juvenile courtrooms; that members of the public enter the room; that arrest and prior record may be reported by the press (from police sources, however, rather than from the juvenile court records); that, once adjudged delinquent, a juvenile may be confined until his majority in what amounts to a prison; and that the stigma attached upon delinquency adjudication approximates that resulting from conviction in an adult criminal proceeding.

The North Carolina juveniles particularly urge that the requirement of a jury trial would not operate to deny the supposed benefits of the juvenile court system; that the system's primary benefits are its discretionary intake procedure permitting disposition short of adjudication, and its flexible sentencing permitting emphasis on rehabilitation; that realization of these benefits does not depend upon dispensing with the jury; that adjudication of factual issues, on the one hand, and disposition of the case, on the other, are very different matters, with very differ-

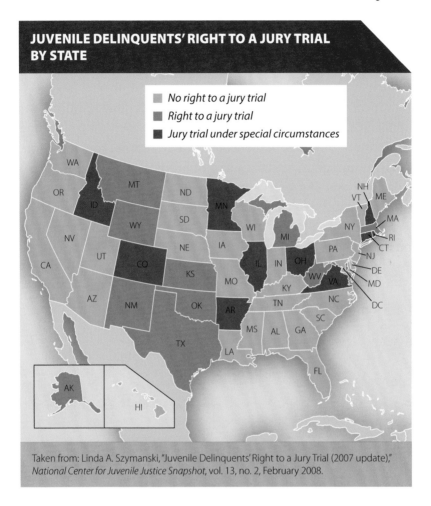

JUVENILE DELINQUENTS' RIGHT TO A JURY TRIAL BY STATE

No right to a jury trial

Right to a jury trial

Jury trial under special circumstances

Taken from: Linda A. Szymanski, "Juvenile Delinquents' Right to a Jury Trial (2007 update)," *National Center for Juvenile Justice Snapshot*, vol. 13, no. 2, February 2008.

ent purposes; that the purpose of the former is indistinguishable from that of the criminal trial; that the jury trial provides an independent protective factor; that experience has shown that jury trials in juvenile courts are manageable; that no reason exists why protection traditionally accorded in criminal proceedings should be denied young people subject to involuntary incarceration for lengthy periods; and that the juvenile courts deserve healthy public scrutiny.

The Jury Concept Is Flexible

All the litigants here agree that the applicable due process standard in juvenile proceedings, as developed by *Gault* and *Winship* [which mandated that juveniles' offenses be proven beyond a reasonable doubt], is fundamental fairness. As that standard was applied in those two cases, we have an emphasis on factfinding procedures. The requirements of notice, counsel, confrontation, cross-examination, and standard of proof naturally flowed from this emphasis. But one cannot say that, in our legal system, the jury is a necessary component of accurate factfinding. There is much to be said for it, to be sure, but we have been content to pursue other ways for determining facts. Juries are not required, and have not been, for example, in equity cases, in workmen's compensation, in probate, or in deportation cases. Neither have they been generally used in military trials. In *Duncan* [*v. Louisiana* (1968)], the Court stated,

> "We would not assert, however, that every criminal trial—or any particular trial—held before a judge alone is unfair, or that a defendant may never be as fairly treated by a judge as he would be by a jury." . . .

And in *Williams v. Florida*, (1970), the Court saw no particular magic in a 12-man jury for a criminal case, thus revealing that even jury concepts themselves are not inflexible.

Juries Could Stifle Juvenile Justice

We must recognize, as the Court has recognized before, that the fond and idealistic hopes of the juvenile court proponents and early reformers of three generations ago have not been realized. The devastating commentary upon the system's failures as a whole, contained in the President's Commission on Law Enforcement and Administration of Justice, Task Force Report: Juvenile Delinquency and Youth Crime 7–9 (1967), reveals the depth of disappointment in what has been accomplished. Too often, the juvenile court judge falls far short of that stalwart, protective, and communicating figure the system envisaged. The community's unwillingness to provide people and facilities and to be concerned, the insufficiency of time devoted, the scarcity of professional help, the inadequacy of dispositional alternatives, and our general lack of knowledge all contribute to dissatisfaction with the experiment.

The Task Force Report, however, also said,

> To say that juvenile courts have failed to achieve their goals is to say no more than what is true of criminal courts in the United States. But failure is most striking when hopes are highest.

Despite all these disappointments, all these failures, and all these shortcomings, we conclude that trial by jury in the juvenile court's adjudicative stage is not a constitutional requirement. We so conclude for a number of reasons:

1. The Court has refrained, in the cases heretofore decided, from taking the easy way with a flat holding that all rights constitutionally assured for the adult accused are to be imposed upon the state juvenile proceeding. What was done in *Gault* and in *Winship* is aptly described in *Commonwealth v. Johnson* (1967):

   > It is clear to us that the Supreme Court has properly attempted to strike a judicious balance by injecting procedural orderliness into the juvenile court system. It is seeking to reverse the trend whereby 'the child receives the worst of both worlds'. . . .

2. There is a possibility, at least, that the jury trial, if required as a matter of constitutional precept, will remake the juvenile proceeding into a fully adversary process and will put an effective end to what has been the idealistic prospect of an intimate, informal protective proceeding.

3. The Task Force Report, although concededly pre-*Gault*, is notable for its not making any recommendation that the jury trial be imposed upon the juvenile court system. This

Because juveniles are not guaranteed a trial by jury, their trials may be held in front of only a judge. © Gaetano/Corbis.

is so despite its vivid description of the system's deficiencies and disappointments. Had the Commission deemed this vital to the integrity of the juvenile process, or to the handling of juveniles, surely a recommendation or suggestion to this effect would have appeared. The intimations, instead, are quite the other way. Further, it expressly recommends against abandonment of the system and against the return of the juvenile to the criminal courts.

4. The Court specifically has recognized by dictum that a jury is not a necessary part even of every criminal process that is fair and equitable.

5. The imposition of the jury trial on the juvenile court system would not strengthen greatly, if at all, the factfinding function, and would, contrarily, provide an attrition of the juvenile court's assumed ability to function in a unique

manner. It would not remedy the defects of the system. Meager as has been the hoped-for advance in the juvenile field, the alternative would be regressive, would lose what has been gained, and would tend once again to place the juvenile squarely in the routine of the criminal process.

Juries Will Not Cure the Ills of the Current System

6. The juvenile concept held high promise. We are reluctant to say that, despite disappointments of grave dimensions, it still does not hold promise, and we are particularly reluctant to say, as do the Pennsylvania appellants here, that the system cannot accomplish its rehabilitative goals. So much depends on the availability of resources, on the interest and commitment of the public, on willingness to learn, and on understanding as to cause and effect and cure. In this field, as in so many others, one perhaps learns best by doing. We are reluctant to disallow the States to experiment further and to seek in new and different ways the elusive answers to the problems of the young, and we feel that we would be impeding that experimentation by imposing the jury trial. The States, indeed, must go forward. If, in its wisdom, any State feels the jury trial is desirable in all cases, or in certain kinds, there appears to be no impediment to its installing a system embracing that feature. That, however, is the State's privilege, and not its obligation.

7. Of course there have been abuses. The Task Force Report has noted them. We refrain from saying at this point that those abuses are of constitutional dimension. They relate to the lack of resources and of dedication, rather than to inherent unfairness.

8. There is, of course, nothing to prevent a juvenile court judge, in a particular case where he feels the need, or when the need is demonstrated, from using an advisory Jury.

States May Mandate Jury Trials for Juveniles

9. "The fact that a practice is followed by a large number of states is not conclusive in a decision as to whether that practice accords with due process, but it is plainly worth considering in determining whether the practice 'offends some principle of justice so rooted in the traditions and conscience of our people as to be ranked as fundamental.' *Snyder v. Massachusetts* (1934)."

    Leland v. Oregon, (1952). It therefore is of more than passing interest that at least 29 States and the District of Columbia by statute deny the juvenile a right to a jury trial in cases such as these. The same result is achieved in other States by judicial decision. In 10 States, statutes provide for a jury trial under certain circumstances.

10. Since *Gault* and since *Duncan,* the great majority of States, in addition to Pennsylvania and North Carolina, that have faced the issue have concluded that the considerations that led to the result in those two cases do not compel trial by jury in the juvenile court.

11. Stopping short of proposing the jury trial for juvenile proceedings are the Uniform Juvenile Court Act, § 24(a), approved in July, 1968, by the National Conference of Commissioners on Uniform State Laws; the Standard Juvenile Court Act, Art. V, § 19, proposed by the National Council on Crime and Delinquency; and the Legislative Guide for Drafting Family and Juvenile Court Acts § 29(a).

Juvenile and Criminal Proceedings Should Remain Separate

12. If the jury trial were to be injected into the juvenile court system as a matter of right, it would bring with it into that system the traditional delay, the formality, and the clamor

of the adversary system and, possibly, the public trial. It is of interest that these very factors were stressed by the District Committee of the Senate when, through Senator [Joseph Davies] Tydings, it recommended, and Congress then approved, as a provision in the District of Columbia Crime Bill, the abolition of the jury trial in the juvenile court.

13. Finally, the arguments advanced by the juveniles here are, of course, the identical arguments that underlie the demand for the jury trial for criminal proceedings. The arguments necessarily equate the juvenile proceeding—or at least the adjudicative phase of it—with the criminal trial. Whether they should be so equated is our issue. Concern about the inapplicability of exclusionary and other rules of evidence, about the juvenile court judge's possible awareness of the juvenile's prior record and of the contents of the social file; about repeated appearances of the same familiar witnesses in the persons of juvenile and probation officers and social workers—all to the effect that this will create the likelihood of pre-judgment—chooses to ignore, it seems to us, every aspect of fairness, of concern, of sympathy, and of paternal attention that the juvenile court system contemplates.

If the formalities of the criminal adjudicative process are to be superimposed upon the juvenile court system, there is little need for its separate existence. Perhaps that ultimate disillusionment will come one day, but, for the moment, we are disinclined to give impetus to it.

> *"The Supreme Court has never contemplated a situation where the juvenile court could impose an adult criminal sentence on the juvenile."*

The Withholding of Jury Trials from Juvenile Offenders Is Outdated in a More Punitive Juvenile Justice System

Katherine Hunt Federle

In the following viewpoint, a law professor argues that the 1971 US Supreme Court ruling in McKeiver v. Pennsylvania *has become outdated. The author claims that current trends suggest youths are receiving harsher punishments than before, and the juvenile justice system is now more apt to impose adult sentences or transfer young offenders to criminal courts. Thus, the author maintains that* McKeiver *unwittingly strips juveniles of a needed right to jury trial. Katherine Hunt Federle is a professor of law at Ohio State University.*

In *McKeiver v. Pennsylvania* [1971], the United States Supreme Court held that the Sixth Amendment right to a jury trial does not apply where a juvenile court may impose only a traditional juvenile disposition. Noting that a juvenile proceeding had never been held to be a criminal prosecution for the purposes of the Sixth Amendment, the plurality in *McKeiver* relied on the Due Process Clause to determine whether a juvenile had a right to a jury trial in a juvenile proceeding. The plurality concluded that there was no such right at the adjudicative stage of a juvenile case because that proceeding is different—more informal, protective, experimental, and promising. Fearing that a jury trial would bring with it the "traditional delay, the formality, and the clamor of the adversary process," the plurality rejected the jury trial as antithetical to the juvenile court's "separate existence." Thus, the jury trial was seen as inconsistent with the juvenile court's rehabilitative goals, providing little in the way of improved fact-finding.

Criminal Justice Goals Have Changed

The Supreme Court's decision in *McKeiver* has had an almost talismanic effect on the lower courts' resolution of a juvenile's right to a jury trial despite the increasingly punitive approach to the treatment of juvenile offenders taken by state legislatures. For example, six states have enacted statutes that explicitly articulate traditional criminal goals, like deterrence, punishment, accountability, and public safety. Another 17 jurisdictions embrace "balanced and restorative justice" principles (including Alabama, Alaska, California, the District of Columbia, Florida, Idaho, Illinois, Indiana, Kansas, Maryland, Minnesota, Montana, New Jersey, Oregon, Pennsylvania, Washington, and Wisconsin) that focus on restoration of the victim through offender accountability while balancing the need to return the offender to law-abiding status. Although many jurisdictions still retain language suggesting rehabilitation as a goal, only three states emphasize the best interests of the child as the primary purpose of the juvenile court. Nevertheless, most state courts have rejected the argument that juveniles in juvenile proceedings have a right to a jury trial as a matter of constitutional law, emphasizing the rehabilitative promise rather than the harsh realities of the juvenile court. Similarly, the federal courts have held that a juvenile has no right to a jury trial in federal delinquency proceedings, relying on *McKeiver.*

States Challenge *McKeiver* As Juvenile Punishments Become More Severe

Nevertheless, some courts have been willing to examine the constitutional issue *McKeiver* seemingly precludes. In *In re L.M.* [2008], the Kansas Supreme Court held that *McKeiver* was no longer binding precedent because legislative changes to the Kansas Juvenile Offender Code "have eroded the benevolent parens patriae [legal doctrine that allows a government to act as a guardian] character that distinguished it from the adult criminal system." The Kansas Supreme Court thus concluded that a minor in a juvenile proceeding has a right to a jury trial under the Sixth and Fourteenth Amendments to the United States Constitution as well as the state constitution. The New Hampshire Supreme Court concluded that the imprisonment of a juvenile in an adult correctional facility was unconstitutional where the juvenile had not first been given a jury trial.

Although the court grounded the right in state constitutional law, the court nevertheless noted that the state's argument that *McKeiver* foreclosed consideration of a right to a jury trial in a juvenile proceeding was inapposite when commitment to an adult criminal institution is permitted.

Although *McKeiver* seemingly precludes further consideration of a juvenile's right to a jury trial in a juvenile proceeding, the structure, purpose, and goals of juvenile courts have changed significantly since the decision was issued over 35 years ago. Since the early 1990s, state legislatures have made sweeping changes to the jurisdictional and dispositional authority of the juvenile courts. Between 1992 and 1997, 44 states and the District of Columbia passed new laws that would send more juveniles to criminal court. Most states simply excluded certain offenders by virtue of age or the charged offense from the juvenile court's original jurisdiction. Twenty-eight states expanded the list of offenses to be excluded from juvenile court jurisdiction, while seven states lowered the age at which a youthful offender could be transferred to criminal court. Some jurisdictions even shifted the burden of proof to the child to rebut the presumption of transfer.

Despite statistical evidence of a significant downturn in juvenile offending, state legislatures continued to amend their transfer laws. Between 1998 and 2002, 31 states enacted amendments to their transfer laws. Of these, 18 states extended their transfer laws, primarily by expanding the number of transfer-eligible offenses. The most dramatic changes occurred in California with the passage of Proposition 21, which created new mechanisms for transfer initiated by prosecutors and new categories of minors excluded from juvenile court jurisdiction. Only six states narrowed their provisions, yet these changes were relatively minor.

The Worrisome Trend of Treating Juveniles As Adults

Currently, every state and the District of Columbia rely on a combination of mechanisms to transfer juveniles to criminal court; these include judicial waiver provisions, direct file laws, and statutory exclusions. Forty-six states have enacted judicial waiver laws in which juvenile court judges enter an order authorizing the transfer of the juvenile to criminal court. Fifteen states have direct file laws that allow the prosecutor to decide whether to file in criminal or juvenile court. An additional 29 states rely on statutory exclusion provisions to exclude certain classes of juveniles from juvenile court jurisdiction *ab initio* [from the outset] while vesting original jurisdiction over these cases in the criminal courts.

But even those juveniles who remain in the juvenile justice system may be subject to criminal penalties. These laws, known as blended sentences, permit juvenile courts to impose adult sanctions on certain qualifying juvenile offenders. To date, 15 states have enacted provisions authorizing juvenile blended sentences. Typically, these laws authorize a juvenile judge to impose a criminal sentence, usually in addition to the juvenile disposition, that the court then suspends on condition that the juvenile successfully complete his juvenile term. In three of these states, however, the court may directly impose an adult sentence in lieu of a juvenile disposition. In three other states, the court has the authority to impose a term of incarceration that may extend years beyond the age limits of the court's jurisdiction without reference to the minor's adjustment or rehabilitation.

In 10 states, the blended sentencing provisions are more expansive than the waiver laws, so more juveniles are at risk of adult sanctions because of these broader eligibility requirements. For example, in some states, the age at which a child may be eligible for a blended sentence is lower than for transfer. Thus, Colorado, Michigan, Rhode Island, and Texas limit the class of juveniles eligible for transfer by requiring that they be of a certain age, but nevertheless permit the imposition of a blended sentence on a child of *any age*. Even juveniles in those states that have expansive waiver provisions may be at higher risk for actual imposition of adult sanctions through the blended sentencing laws. Because once a minor has been waived to criminal court, he or she will be treated as an adult for all subsequent criminal prosecutions in most jurisdictions. Waiver is generally an irrevocable and final decision; thus, the decision to pursue a blended sentence may be a way to reach juveniles who would not otherwise warrant transfer.

Harsh Punishments Seem to Necessitate Jury Trials

The Supreme Court has never contemplated a situation where the juvenile court could impose an adult criminal sentence on

Some legal scholars argue that juveniles should have the right to a trial by jury as seen in this courtroom. © David Frazier/Stone/Getty Images.

the juvenile since no statute or other analogous procedure existed in any state at the time *McKeiver* was decided. Accordingly, *McKeiver* does not address whether a minor who is given a criminal sentence of imprisonment for a term of years is entitled to a jury trial as a constitutional matter. *McKeiver* thus has served to bar a critical examination of the assumptions about the juvenile justice system and the rights of juveniles to such an extent that when a minor receives an adult prison term, he or she is not afforded the protections of the Sixth Amendment.

Consequently, the Supreme Court has never had the opportunity to consider the extent to which *Apprendi v. New Jersey* [2000], *Blakely v. Washington* [2004], and their progeny apply to juvenile court proceedings where the minor may receive a prison term in addition to a traditional juvenile disposition. In *Apprendi v. New Jersey*, the Court held that with the sole exception of prior convictions of the defendant, any fact that increases the penalty for a crime beyond the statutorily prescribed maximum must be submitted to a jury. In *Blakely v. Washington*, the Court held that the maximum sentence a judge may impose must rest "*solely on the basis of the facts reflected in the jury verdict or admitted by the defendant.*" Moreover, any judicial fact-finding raises constitutional issues; any fact that elevates a sentence beyond the statutory maximum allowed by a finding of guilt or a guilty plea must be found by the jury. Thus, the Supreme Court made clear that to impose a sentence greater than the statutory maximum, without the necessary factual findings from the jury that would warrant an enhanced sentence, violates the defendant's right to a jury trial under the Sixth Amendment to the United States Constitution.

The Ohio Case Under Review

However, the Supreme Court is considering a petition for a writ of certiorari [judicial review] to the Ohio Supreme Court on this very issue. Pursuant to Ohio law, minors tried in juvenile court in cases designated as serious youthful offender (SYO) proceedings, may receive a blended sentence: a traditional juvenile disposition in addition to a stayed adult prison sentence (a "discretionary SYO sentence"). Prior to imposing a discretionary SYO sentence, the juvenile court is required to make a finding on the record that:

> given the nature and circumstances of the violation and the history of the child, the length of time, level of security and types of programming and resources available in the juvenile system alone are not adequate to provide the juvenile court with a reasonable expectation that the purposes set forth in section 2152.01 of Revised Code will be met. . . .

The statute provides that after that finding is made, "the juvenile court may impose upon the child a sentence available for the violation, as if the child were an adult, under Chapter 2929 of the Revised Code. . . ." Such prison sentences can be lengthy and are indistinguishable from sentences imposed on adult offenders.

Ohio's discretionary SYO provisions appear to require exactly the type of judicial fact-finding prohibited by *Apprendi* and *Blakely*. Petitioner, D.H., was sentenced by a juvenile court judge to serve a traditional juvenile disposition as well as a criminal prison sentence of six years, the latter sentence stayed pending "successful completion" of the juvenile disposition. The juvenile court's imposition of a criminal prison sentence, however, exceeded the maximum term a juvenile court may ordinarily impose. The Ohio Supreme Court nevertheless concluded that no Sixth Amendment right was contravened because *McKeiver* held that the Sixth Amendment does not apply to juvenile court proceedings. Thus, without further discussion of the Sixth Amendment issue, the Ohio Supreme Court concluded that the statutory procedures did not violate the Due Process Clause of the Fourteenth Amendment.

The minor petitioner in *D.H. v. Ohio* [2006] raises a novel constitutional claim in his petition for certiorari: that the imposition of an adult sentence in addition to a traditional juvenile disposition enhances the sentence beyond the statutory maximum and thus violates the principles articulated in *Apprendi*, *Blakely*, and their progeny where the necessary factual findings to enhance the sentence are not made by the jury. The claim is made all the more compelling because the petitioner is not suggesting he did not receive a jury trial: He in fact was tried by a jury in the state juvenile court. Rather, petitioner alleges that the juvenile court's decision to impose a criminal sentence beyond the juvenile disposition triggers certain constitutional protections under the Sixth Amendment and that the imposition of the adult sentence violates *Apprendi* and *Blakely*. The Ohio State University Justice for Children Project has filed an amicus brief in support of the petitioner, arguing that the Supreme Court should grant the petition because of the significance of the case, given the novelty of the constitutional claims and the questionable validity of *McKeiver* in light of the changing face of the juvenile justice system. This case thus represents an important opportunity for the Supreme Court to revisit the extent to which juveniles have constitutional rights in cases where their treatment varies little from that of criminal defendants.

> *"Children who knowingly engage in adult conduct and adult crimes should automatically be subject to adult rules and adult prison time."*

Juveniles Should Be Tried As Adults When They Have Committed Violent Crimes

Linda J. Collier

In the following viewpoint, a lawyer argues that the juvenile justice system is behind the times in addressing violent youth crimes. She contends the system was originally designed to rehabilitate young people committing petty offenses. The author believes that the numerous school shootings, rapes, and other violent crimes perpetrated by modern youth are signs that the juvenile justice system is failing in its rehabilitative mission. She insists that states must reform their juvenile justice laws. Linda J. Collier is a Pennsylvania lawyer who has dealt with numerous juvenile justice cases.

When prosecutor Brent Davis said he wasn't sure if he could charge 11-year-old Andrew Golden and 13-year-old Mitchell Johnson as adults after Tuesday afternoon's slaughter in

Jonesboro, Ark., I cringed.[1] But not for the reasons you might think.

I knew he was formulating a judgment based on laws that have not had a major overhaul for more than 100 years. I knew his hands were tied by the longstanding creed that juvenile offenders, generally defined as those under the age of 18, are to be treated rather than punished. I knew he would have to do legal cartwheels to get the case out of the juvenile system. But most of all, I cringed because today's juvenile suspects—even those who are accused of committing the most violent crimes—are still regarded by the law as children first and criminals second.

Younger Assailants Are Committing More Violent Crimes

As astonishing as the Jonesboro events were, this is hardly the first time that children with access to guns and other weapons have brought tragedy to a school. Only weeks before the Jonesboro shootings, three girls in Paducah, Ky., were killed in their school lobby when a 14-year-old classmate allegedly opened fire on them. Authorities said he had several guns with him, and the alleged murder weapon was one of seven stolen from a neighbor's garage. And the day after the Jonesboro shootings, a 14-year-old in Daly City, Calif., was charged as a juvenile after he allegedly fired at his middle-school principal with a semiautomatic handgun.

It's not a new or unusual phenomenon for children to commit violent crimes at younger and younger ages, but it often takes a shocking incident to draw our attention to a trend already in progress. According to the U.S. Department of Justice, crimes committed by juveniles have increased by 60 percent since 1984. Where juvenile delinquency was once limited to truancy or vandalism, juveniles now are more likely to be the perpetrators of serious and deadly crimes such as arson, aggravated assault, rape and murder. And these violent offenders increasingly include those as young as the Jonesboro suspects. Since 1965, the

Areas of Westside Middle School in Jonesboro, Arkansas, were cordoned off following a shooting at the school in 1998. Some believe that juveniles should be tried as adults for especially violent crimes like this shooting. © Leigh Daughtridge/The Commercial Appeal/Landov.

number of 12-year-olds arrested for violent crimes has doubled and the number of 13- and 14-year-olds has tripled, according to government statistics.

Those statistics are a major reason why we need to revamp our antiquated juvenile justice system. Nearly every state, including Arkansas, has laws that send most youthful violent offenders to the juvenile courts, where they can only be found "delinquent" and confined in a juvenile facility (typically not past age 21). In recent years, many states have enacted changes in their juvenile crime laws, and some have lowered the age at which a juvenile can be tried as an adult for certain violent crimes. Virginia, for example, has reduced its minimum age to 14, and suspects accused of murder and aggravated malicious wounding are automatically waived to adult court. Illinois is now sending some 13-year-olds to adult court after a hearing in juvenile court. In Kansas, a 1996 law allows juveniles as young as 10 to be prosecuted as adults in some cases. These are steps in the right direction, but too many states still treat violent offenders under 16 as juveniles who belong in the juvenile system.

A System Not Geared Toward Violent Offenders

My views are not those of a frustrated prosecutor. I have represented children as a court-appointed guardian ad litem, or temporary guardian, in the Philadelphia juvenile justice system. Loosely defined, a guardian ad litem is responsible for looking after the best interest of a neglected or rebellious child who has come into the juvenile courts. It is often a humbling experience as I try to help children whose lives have gone awry, sometimes because of circumstances beyond their control.

My experience has made me believe that the system is doing a poor job at treatment as well as punishment. One of my "girls," a chronic truant, was a foster child who longed to be adopted. She often talked of how she wanted a pink room, a frilly bunk bed and sisters with whom she could share her dreams. She languished in foster care from ages 2 to 13 because her drug-ravaged mother would not relinquish her parental rights. Initially, the girl refused to tolerate the half-life that the state had maintained was in her best interest. But as it became clear that we would never convince her mother to give up her rights, the girl became a frequent runaway. Eventually she ended up pregnant, wandering from place to place and committing adult crimes to survive. No longer a child, not quite a woman, she is the kind of teenager offender for whom the juvenile system has little or nothing to offer.

A brief history: Proceedings in juvenile justice began in 1890 in Chicago, where the original mandate was to save wayward children and protect them from the ravages of society. The system called for children to be processed through an appendage of the family court. By design, juveniles were to be kept away from the court's criminal side, the district attorney and adult correctional institutions.

Typically, initial procedures are informal, non-threatening and not open to public scrutiny. A juvenile suspect is interviewed by an "intake" officer who determines the child's fate. The intake officer may issue a warning, lecture and release; he may detain the suspect; or, he may decide to file a petition, subjecting the child to juvenile "adjudication" proceedings. If the law allows, the intake officer may make a recommendation that the juvenile be transferred to adult criminal court.

An adjudication is similar to a hearing, rather than a trial, although the juvenile may be represented by counsel and a juvenile prosecutor will represent the interests of the community. It is important to note that throughout the proceedings, no matter which side of the fence the parties are on, the operating principle is that everyone is working in the best interests of the child. Juvenile court judges do not issue findings of guilt, but decide whether a child is delinquent. If delinquency is found, the judge must decide the child's fate. Should the child be sent back to the family—assuming there is one? Declare him or her "in need of supervision," which brings in the intense help of social services? Remove the child from the family and place him or her in foster care? Confine the child to a state institution for juvenile offenders?

This system was developed with truants, vandals and petty thieves in mind. But this model is not appropriate for the violent juvenile offender of today. Detaining a rapist or murderer in a juvenile facility until the age of 18 or 21 isn't even a slap on the hand. If a juvenile is accused of murdering, raping or assaulting someone with a deadly weapon, the suspect should automatically be sent to adult criminal court. What's to ponder?

A Mandate Is Needed for Trying Kids As Adults

With violent crime becoming more prevalent among the junior set, it's a mystery why there hasn't been a major overhaul of juvenile justice laws long before now. Will the Jonesboro shootings

SENTENCING THIRTEEN- AND FOURTEEN-YEAR-OLDS TO DIE IN PRISON

■ States that have sentenced thirteen- or fourteen-year-olds to life in prison without parole

Taken from: Equal Justice Initiative, *Cruel and Unusual: Sentencing 13- and 14-Year-Old Children to Die in Prison*. Montgomery, AL: Equal Justice Initiative, January 2008.

be the incident that makes us take a hard look at the current system? When it became evident that the early release of Jesse Timmendequas—whose murder of 7-year-old Megan Kanka in New Jersey sparked national outrage—had caused unwarranted tragedy, legislative action was swift. Now New Jersey has Megan's Law, which requires the advance notification of a sexual predator's release into a neighborhood. Other states have followed suit.

It is unequivocally clear that the same type of mandate is needed to establish a uniform minimum age for trying juveniles as adults. As it stands now, there is no consistency in state laws governing waivers to adult court. One reason for this lack of uniformity is the absence of direction from the federal government or Congress. The Bureau of Justice Statistics reports that adjacent states such as New York and Pennsylvania respond differently to 16-year-old criminals, with New York tending to treat offenders of that age as adults and Pennsylvania handling them in the juvenile justice system.

Federal prosecution of juveniles is not totally unheard of, but it is uncommon. The Bureau of Justice Statistics estimates that during 1994, at least 65 juveniles were referred to the attorney general for transfer to adult status. In such cases, the U.S. attorney's office must certify a substantial federal interest in the case and show that one of the following is true: The state does not have jurisdiction; the state refuses to assume jurisdiction or the state does not have adequate services for juvenile offenders; the offense is a violent felony, drug trafficking or firearm offense as defined by the U.S. Code.

Exacting hurdles, but not insurmountable. In the Jonesboro case, prosecutor Davis has been exploring ways to enlist the federal court's jurisdiction. Whatever happens, federal prosecutions of young offenders are clearly not the long-term answer. The states must act. So as far as I can see, the next step is clear: Children who knowingly engage in adult conduct and adult crimes should automatically be subject to adult rules and adult prison time.

Note

1. On March 24, 1998, Johnson and Golden shot fifteen students and teachers at Westside Middle School. One teacher and four students died from wounds; one teacher and nine other students were injured.

> *"Adolescents are not small adults, and should not be treated or punished as if they were."*

Juveniles Should Not Be Tried or Sentenced As Adults

Patrick T. McCormick

In the following viewpoint, a Christian ethics professor claims that more juvenile offenders are being remanded to the adult criminal courts system. The author believes this is an injustice and a moral tragedy. He contends that the juvenile justice system was devised with the understanding that young people are not mature enough to grasp the consequences of their actions. He regrets that this legal understanding has dissipated in modern times and given way to an overriding notion that the punishment must fit the crime without consideration for the rehabilitative capacity of youth. Patrick T. McCormick is a professor of Christian ethics at Gonzaga University in Spokane, Washington.

Imagine a 12-year-old boy who has committed a brutal, senseless homicide. Now imagine a 47-year-old legislator who claims this child should be treated as if he were a mature adult. Which of these is behaving like a grown-up? Last year [in 2001] prosecutors in Florida put two 14-year-olds on trial as adults for homicides committed when the youngsters were 12 and 13 years of age. A Fort Lauderdale jury convicted Lionel Tate of first-degree murder in the 1999 death of 6-year-old Tiffany Eunick, and the judge imposed a mandatory sentence of life without parole. Four months later a West Palm Beach jury found Nathaniel Brazill guilty of second-degree murder and the 14-year-old was sentenced to 28 years in prison without parole for killing his English teacher, Barry Grunow. Meanwhile, a superior court in California has ruled that 15-year-old Charles Andrew Williams should be tried as an adult for the murder of two students in a school shooting last March.

In these states we would not let a 12- or 13-year-old buy a carton of cigarettes, a six-pack of beer or a ticket to the movie "American Pie 2." They are not mature, competent or responsible enough to drive a car, get a job, move out of the house, marry, serve in the military or vote. They need a note from their parents to go on a class trip to the zoo. But let a 12-year-old do something truly monstrous, and suddenly state and federal lawmakers want to behave as if this child were competent to stand trial as an adult in a capital murder case—as if it made sense to punish this prepubescent adolescent in the same way we would a hardened felon.

And Masters Tate, Brazill and Williams are just the tip of the iceberg. Over the past decade legislators in 47 states and the District of Columbia have made it easier to put on trial and punish juveniles as adults. Between 1985 and 1997 the number of minors admitted to state prisons more than doubled, climbing from 3,400 to 7,400. In 1998 U.S. jails housed nearly 7,000 youngsters awaiting trial, and prisons and adult correctional facilities held more than 11,000 juveniles. That same year state and federal prosecutors charged 200,000 young people with criminal offenses.

The Principles of Juvenile Justice

Children in U.S. prisons or jails are not a new phenomenon. Before 19th-century reformers established America's first juvenile court in Chicago in 1899, children who had reached the age of reason (7) were often tried and sentenced along with adults, serving time in the same prisons and occasionally facing execution. In the period from 1870 to 1890, one out of every 25 convicts in San Quentin and Folsom prisons was between 14 and 17.

But for most of the past century, juvenile courts and correction facilities have treated youngsters between 7 and 17 not as criminals but as delinquents, and (in theory at least) focused on rehabilitating the youthful offender rather than punishing the offense. Unlike criminal courts, the proceedings here were not adversarial, but informal and confidential. And juveniles were not convicted or sent to prison, but adjudicated delinquent and put on probation or sent to training schools or reformatories.

Two underlying beliefs have guided the practice of these juvenile courts: first, that children and adolescents are not responsible for their actions in the same way as adults; and second, that they are more open to reform and rehabilitation than their elders. Because of the immaturity and malleability of juveniles, their guilt was weighed differently, and rehabilitation took priority over punishment.

But not all juveniles were kept out of criminal court. Judges in juvenile courts could transfer youths who were nearly 18, habitual offenders or guilty of particularly serious crimes, and down through the years about 1 percent of youthful offenders were sent to adult court by means of these judicial waivers.

But in the early 1990s, legislators in nearly every state responded to concerns about a spike in juvenile violent crime rates and began tinkering with the juvenile justice system, making it easier to put more and younger adolescents on trial as adults and to send them to adult jails and prisons—sometimes for life, occasionally for death. State and federal lawmakers made a number of changes in the juvenile justice system. They expanded judicial waivers, allowing judges to transfer younger and less serious offenders to adult court, and they increased the number of cases in which judges are presumed or mandated to issue waiv-

Transferring Juveniles to Adult Courts Increases Recidivism

> To date, six large-scale studies have been conducted on the specific deterrent effects of transfer. . . . All of the studies found higher recidivism rates among offenders who had been transferred to criminal court, compared with those who were retained in the juvenile system. This held true even for offenders who only received a sentence of probation from the criminal court. Thus, the extant research provides sound evidence that transferring juvenile offenders to the criminal court does not engender community protection by reducing recidivism. On the contrary, transfer substantially increases recidivism.
>
> *Richard E. Redding, "Juvenile Transfer Laws:*
> *An Effective Deterrent to Delinquency?," Office*
> *of Juvenile Justice and Delinquency Prevention*
> Juvenile Justice Bulletin, *June 2010.*

ers. They gave prosecutors new or expanded authority to file charges against minors in criminal court, passed legislation excluding certain offenses from juvenile courts and in some states even lowered the age at which all juveniles must be sent to adult court. They also introduced blended sentences, allowing juvenile offenders to finish the last years or decades of their term in adult prisons. And they demanded mandatory minimum sentences for a variety of juvenile offenses.

Fears Mount As Crime Rates Drop

As it turns out, the surge in juvenile violent crime rates that began in the late 1980s was already ending as legislators made these changes, and could have been better dealt with by limiting adolescents' access to handguns. These, at least, were the findings of a recent report by the Sentencing Project, a Washington-based research group, titled *Prosecuting Juveniles in Adult Court.* Still, shaken by stories of "superpredators" and school shootings, lawmakers decided to get tough on juvenile crime and shift the focus from rehabilitating offenders to punishing offenses. As a result, the vast majority of states now allow 14-year-olds to be tried as adults. Fifteen states explicitly permit this practice for children as young as 13, 12 or 10. And more than half the states have one offense for which juveniles of any age can be charged as adults. At the same time, 38 states house juveniles in the general population in adult prisons or jails.

Still, our toughness on juveniles is not limited to this new willingness to try and punish more and younger children as adults. America's judicial system can also boast an uncommon and unpopular readiness to sentence juveniles to life, or death. The Convention on the Rights of the Child, an international treaty ratified by every U.N. member except the United States and Somalia, forbids punishing any crime committed by a minor with life imprisonment without parole. But in 1998 California had 14 prisoners serving this sentence for crimes committed when they were 16 or 17. And, of course, Lionel Tate just received this punishment for a crime he committed as a 12-year-old.

Meanwhile, as we saw in all the furor last August over the Texas inmate Napoleon Beazley, America remains one of a handful of countries that execute juvenile offenders. At 17, Beazley murdered John Luttig, and at 25 he was scheduled to become the 19th person executed in the United States since 1976 for a crime committed as a minor. Sentencing juvenile offenders to death is in clear violation of a number of U.N. conventions and treaties and has been condemned by the American Bar Association, most major religious denominations and just about every human rights group with a Web site. Even China gave up the practice in 1997. Still, the U.S. Supreme Court has upheld the constitutionality of executing people over 16, and 23 states currently allow capital punishment for juveniles. [In the 2005 case *Roper v. Simmons,* the court disallowed capital punishment for juveniles under eighteen.] So approximately 80 U.S. prisoners sit on death row waiting to be executed for crimes they committed at 16 or 17, and in the last decade over half of the world's executions of juvenile offenders have been in the United States. More than half of those were carried out in Texas.

Nonviolent Offenses Can Still Land Juveniles in Adult Court

From all the media attention given to cases like those of Beazley, Tate, Brazill and Williams, it would be easy to conclude that the vast majority of juveniles being tried as adults are violent offenders, probably murderers. But, in [songwriter Ira] Gershwin's phrase, it ain't necessarily so. In both 1995 and 1996 fewer than half the cases nationwide waived to criminal court involved violence against people. And a study released in October 2000, *Youth Crime/Adult Time*, found that current laws cast too wide a net, sending many juveniles into adult courts and jails for nonviolent offenses. According to the study, nearly 40 percent of the juveniles tried as adults were charged with nonviolent crimes, and many were not convicted or were sent back to juvenile court, which suggests that their cases were neither strong nor serious. "The findings suggest that the adult criminal court is taking on numerous cases that should be prosecuted in the juvenile justice system."

Ironically enough, legislators and prosecutors are charging and punishing more and more juveniles as adults at the very moment researchers are confirming just how different adolescents are from grown-ups. According to a report this year by a National Research Council panel, titled *Juvenile Crime, Juvenile Justice*, children and adolescents think, feel and judge differently than adults—often overestimating their grasp of a situation and underestimating the negative consequences of their actions.

Recent brain studies indicate that children and adolescents process emotionally charged information in that part of the brain responsible for instinct and gut reaction, while adults do

Rena and Ireland Beazley (left to right) hold a photo of their son Napoleon, one of the last juveniles executed prior to a 2004 US Supreme Court decision abolishing the death penalty for minors. © AP Images/Donna McWilliam.

this work in the more "rational" frontal section. Other research shows that while strong emotions can cloud or distort judgments for both adults and adolescents, teens experience wider and more frequent mood swings. All of this suggests that juveniles lack the cognitive and emotional maturity of adults, are less able to think rationally or clearly when faced with emotionally charged decisions and should be held less culpable for their choices.

At the same time, studies of juvenile defendants raise questions about their capacity to grasp the adversarial process of criminal court and their competence to stand trial as adults. Youngsters under 15 often misunderstand their legal rights and are more likely to confess in detail to an authority figure. Children find it more difficult to remember or recount events in a consistent or coherent fashion. They often forget names, addresses and the correct sequence of events, making it more difficult for them to assist in their defense and easier for police or prosecutors to discredit their testimony. On the witness stand children often appear unemotional and callous, even though they are deeply frightened or upset. And when faced with plea offers from the prosecution, juveniles have a poor grasp of the strength of the case against them or the long-term consequences of their decision. When Nathaniel Brazill realized he was facing a prison sentence of more than a quarter-century, his response was, "Not too bad"—hardly an indication that he understood what was going on.

The Dangers of Jail Time

And if it is a mistake to put juveniles on trial as adults, it may be a greater one to incarcerate them with grown-ups. Adolescents in adult jails and prisons are more vulnerable to a wide range of dangers. Compared with youngsters in juvenile detention centers, youths housed in adult jails are nearly eight times as likely to commit suicide. They are five times as likely to be sexually assaulted, and twice as likely to be beaten by staff members. And they are 50 percent more likely to be attacked with a weapon. A story in the *Miami Herald* suggests that youngsters in Florida prisons are nearly 21 times as likely to report being assaulted or injured as adolescents in the state's juvenile justice system.

Nor does treating juveniles as adults make our communities or society any safer. About 80 percent of juveniles admitted to prison are released before their 21st birthday, and being jailed with adults does not seem to discourage them from returning to a life of crime. If anything, the opposite may be true. Studies in Florida, Pennsylvania, New York and New Jersey and a good deal of national research indicate that recidivism rates are higher among juveniles who are transferred to adult court than among those who remain in the juvenile system. Adolescents who are tried and punished as adults are more likely to offend again, to do so sooner and more often, and to commit more serious crimes than those kept in juvenile court. States like Florida that prosecute large numbers of juveniles as adults have some of the highest juvenile violent-crime rates. And even deterrence programs like Scared Straight, which sought to deter juvenile offenders by exposing them briefly to prison life and adult convicts, have been an unmitigated disaster and led to increased criminal behavior on the part of adolescents.

Indeed, the evidence suggests that several community-based programs that do not involve imprisonment are both less costly and more effective than trying and punishing adolescents as adults. As the authors of *Juvenile Crime, Juvenile Justice* note, "Research has shown that treating most juvenile offenders within the community does not compromise public safety and may even improve it through reduced recidivism."

In their pastoral statement last year on crime and criminal justice, the U.S. Catholic bishops came out against "policies that treat young offenders as though they are adults." According to the bishops, "society must never respond to children who have committed crimes as though they are somehow equal to adults—fully formed in conscience and fully aware of their actions." It would be a mistake to think that the bishops (or the Catholic moral tradition, for that matter) are soft on crime, or do not hold persons morally responsible for their actions. As they note elsewhere, "we believe in responsibility, accountability and legitimate punishment. Those who harm others or damage property must be held accountable for the hurt they have caused." Still, "not everyone has the same ability to exercise free will, [and] each person is responsible for and will be judged by his or her actions *according to the potential that has been given to him or her*" (emphasis added). . . .

More than a century after the first juvenile court was founded in Chicago, we have even more reason to know that adolescents are not small adults, and should not be treated or punished as if they were. . . . Developmental psychology has confirmed what Shakespeare told us long ago, that we go through several stages in our cognitive, affective and moral development, and that between the adult and the infant is the "whining school-boy" or adolescent. If we are to play the part of mature adults (Shakespeare's judge), we will need to know the differences between these stages and act accordingly.

> *"No child should be placed with adults
> no matter what, because when children
> are put in with adults they die—
> physically or mentally."*

The Mother of a Son Incarcerated in an Adult Prison Tells Why the System Fails Young People

Personal Narrative

Tracy McClard

In the following viewpoint, the mother of a son incarcerated in an adult prison relates his experience of fighting to survive in the violent environment. The author asserts that her son earned the praise of youth service administrators who believed he was a good candidate for a program that allowed youth to serve time in a separate facility. However, she claims the presiding judge ignored the recommendation and ordered her son back to jail. Tracy McClard is the mother of Jonathan McClard, who in 2007 began serving time at age sixteen for shooting the boyfriend of his former girlfriend.

Tracy McClard, Testimony, Hearing on "Reforming the Juvenile Justice System to Improve Children's Lives and Public Safety," House Committee on Education and Labor, April 21, 2010.

My name is Tracy McClard and I live in Jackson, MO. In 2008, I lost my barely 17-year-old son, Jonathan, in Missouri's criminal justice system.

Impact of Jail Time on Young Offenders

Before I begin telling my family's experience with having our son in the adult criminal justice system, I would like to give you some data to help put our story into context. Each year, an estimated 200,000 youth go into the adult criminal court and every day 10,000 kids under the age of 18 are incarcerated in adult jails and prisons.

These policies exist even though research shows that prosecuting children as adults causes harm to these youth and does not increase public safety. Reports from the Office of Juvenile Justice and Delinquency Prevention (OJJDP) and the Centers for Disease Control and Prevention (CDC)'s non-federal Task Force on Community Preventive Services, show that prosecuting youth as adults actually increases crime. The CDC report found that youth involved in the adult system are 34% more likely to commit crimes than children who have done similar crimes, but remain in the juvenile justice system. The OJJDP report found that prosecuting youth as adults increases the chances of a youth re-offending and recommended decreasing the number of youth in the adult criminal justice system.

Research also shows that youth in adult jails face unbelievable conditions. First, these youth are at great risk of physical and sexual assault. The National Prison Rape Elimination Commission recently found that "more than any other group of incarcerated persons, youth incarcerated with adults are probably at the highest risk for sexual abuse" and said youth be housed separately from adults. Second, youth in jails typically do not have access to things like education, mental health programs, or substance abuse treatment, especially when compared to kids in juvenile facilities. Finally, and as my family tragically knows too well, youth in adult jails are at a high risk of suicide: youth in adult jails are 36 times more likely to complete suicide in an adult jail than youth juvenile detention facilities.

An Act of Poor Judgment

In July 2007, my son Jonathan, who was 16 years old at the time, made an extremely poor error in judgment. That morning Jonathan's ex-girlfriend called to tell him that she was pregnant with Jonathan's baby, but that her new boyfriend was abusive and was going to force her to inject cocaine and kill the baby. She also told him she was going to commit suicide before the new boyfriend could do this. Under the influence of drugs, and in what he thought was an attempt to save two lives, Jonathan shot the boyfriend, who survived, with the intent to scare him into leaving the ex-girlfriend alone. Thinking the police would understand why he did what he did and not understanding the gravity of his actions, Jonathan immediately turned himself in. While I believed that Jonathan needed to be held accountable for his actions as well as pay retribution, I never would have imagined the conditions he would face in the adult criminal justice system that ultimately took his life.

A Tumultuous Journey

Our ordeal began with Jonathan being taken to an adolescent psychiatric hospital in St. Louis, MO within two hours of his arrest due to shock and suicidal thoughts in the aftermath of the event. The charge nurse there said that Jonathan was very confused and afraid. He remained in that facility for two weeks and was then ultimately transferred to the Cape Girardeau Juvenile Detention Center to be closer to home.

While in the psychiatric hospital, Jonathan was prescribed an extremely high amount of anti-psychotic medication. When he was transferred back to the juvenile facilities we, as his parents, had no control over Jonathan's medication or the dosage. It took several weeks for his body to adjust and during this time he had recurring nightmares about the loss of his baby and hallucinations of blood running down the walls. Eventually his body adjusted to the medication. In the juvenile detention center, Jonathan was allowed to complete homework from school and stay caught up. Jonathan remained in the Cape Girardeau County Juvenile Detention Center until September 6, 2007.

On that day, Jonathan had a certification hearing where he was transferred to the adult system. At the conclusion of the hearing he was immediately placed in the Cape Girardeau County Jail with adults in Jackson, MO. He was a 140 lb., slight built, 16-year-old child among much older, bigger men. As soon as he arrived, all the medication he was forced to take earlier was abruptly stopped due to the jail's anti-narcotics policies, causing intense withdrawal symptoms, including shaking, another bout of hallucinations and severe depression. There was no medical care, medication or concern on the part of the jail's staff as Jonathan was forced to suffer these withdrawal symptoms.

At the jail, the ability for Jonathan to continue his education was also put on hold. Because he was now in the adult system, his school was no longer required to send homework and he was officially dropped from their roster. This was really difficult for Jonathan to deal with as he loved school, learning, reading and research. He had a lot of friends, made good grades and his teachers really enjoyed having him in class. He was working toward scholarships and had plans to become a doctor or psychiatrist. In the weeks waiting for his certification hearing, he mentioned several times how worried he was about his education. The night before the hearing he said, "I wonder if my teachers know I have to go to jail tomorrow and I can't be in school anymore. My life is over."

In order to continue with his education, Jonathan tried to work on a GED [General Educational Development] book, but he told me that it was too noisy in the jail and nobody was there to help or support him. He ended up staring at the TV every day and at night he could not sleep as the lights were kept on and the adult inmates stayed up. He waited to use the restroom and take a shower in the mid-morning hours when the other inmates were sleeping to avoid being assaulted. Jonathan spent approximately two weeks in the Cape Girardeau County Jail and due to a change in venue was then transferred to the Mississippi County Jail in Charleston, MO.

Powerless to Help

I knew the transfer was coming, I just didn't know when. Due to security protocol, families are not allowed to know when loved ones are being moved. Before Jonathan was transferred, I called the Mississippi County Jail to speak to the supervisor about his safety. The supervisor led me to believe he was very concerned about having someone so young in his jail, that he would be very careful about which pod he chose to place Jonathan, and that other inmates had been singled out to watch over him. I was told that the officers would keep an eye out for him and he would be fine.

Jonathan was transferred on a Thursday. We were allowed only one 15-minute visit a week, either on Monday or Thursday between one and four o'clock. My husband and I took time away from our jobs each week to visit. We visited through glass by talking on a phone. Since Jonathan was moved on Thursday, the following Monday was our first opportunity to see him.

As Jonathan approached his side of the glass, my husband and I were shocked by what we saw. Jonathan had cuts and bruises all over his face, ears, and head. His hair was shaved off and he had a tattoo under his eye. He was told by the other inmates in the facility he needed the tattoo to survive. I immediately broke down and wept because I was utterly powerless to keep him safe. As I questioned him about what happened, I learned that he was attacked the night he arrived there. He said there was a meth lab in the jail and the person who attacked him was someone he shared a cell with and who was coming down off of meth. This person took Jonathan's shirt and pulled it over his head so he couldn't see and so his arms were trapped. Jonathan kept trying to reassure me

Incarcerating Juvenile Offenders as Adults

One of the most striking examples of the disconnect between juvenile justice means and ends is adultification—that is, trying minors in adult court and sentencing them to adult prisons. About 200,000 minors enter the adult criminal justice system each year. Research on minors sent to the adult system says that they are more likely to re-offend and escalate into violent behavior than their peers who go to the juvenile system, where rehabilitative services are far more extensive. We also know that youths in adult prisons are at high risk for suicide and for victimization by adult inmates. . . .

Youth crime was already declining as many adultification laws were passed. Today, youth violence is at a 30-year low. But the public perception remains that juvenile crime is escalating.

Colleen Shaddox, "Juvenile Justice and the Theater of the Absurd," Miller-McCune, *November 4, 2008. www.miller-mccune.com.*

that he would be okay and this was his fault because he'd gotten himself into this nightmare. We both knew he wouldn't be okay.

Following the extremely short visit, Jonathan was led back into the madhouse and my husband and I sought out the supervisor that I had spoken with on the phone. When we asked about the events of the fight and Jonathan's promised safety a very unconcerned supervisor told us, "Things like this happen! What do you expect? We don't tolerate fighting of any sort so if Jonathan participates in it again he'll be placed in solitary confinement. I don't care what the circumstances are."

Surviving in a Violent Environment

On our next visit a week later, Jonathan was visibly shaken. He said, "Mom this place is so scary." I asked what happened. He described an incident that happened that week of a new inmate coming in. He said when this man was brought in several inmates grabbed him and dragged him to the back. He said, "Mom, I could hear him screaming and screaming and nobody did anything! When they brought him back out I couldn't recognize him because he was so bloody and beat up and he got sent to solitary, but nobody else got into trouble."

For the next several visits, Jonathan always had stories to tell about violent things that happened that week and comments he was hearing from inmates who had been to prison about how to survive if he had to go to prison. He was constantly trying to strengthen his body to survive present and future attacks. He talked about how he was told he needed to be in a gang, which he didn't want to join, to survive. At this point, he was trying to decide between making education a priority and dealing with the bullying and beating that came with studying for the GED or if he should forget his education so he could join a gang and be safer. Jonathan remained in the Mississippi County Jail until his sentencing hearing on November 13, 2007.

Blended Sentencing Program Offers Hope

Missouri has a blended sentencing option in place called the Missouri Dual Jurisdiction Program, which is run by the Missouri Department of Youth Services (DYS) and serves youth up to age 21 who have been certified as adults. Youth sentenced to this program are placed in a secure facility near St. Louis and are allowed to live in dorm style rooms, wear their own clothes, and have their own possessions from home. They also receive their high school diploma or GED, can take college classes, and have extensive individual and group counseling geared toward substance abuse, positive choices, victim empathy and restoration and other issues geared toward this specific population. Families are also encouraged to visit and remain involved. To be allowed into this program, a youth is interviewed by the DYS and a recommendation is given to the judge for acceptance or rejection. If accepted, the adult sentence is suspended while the youth receives intensive counseling and education. At the age of 21, another hearing is scheduled to decide if the youth can go home on probation or if the youth must serve the rest of the sentence in the adult prison. The decision for initial placement and adult placement is ultimately up to the judge.

Jonathan was interviewed for this program and was highly recommended. A representative from the DYS came to his sentencing hearing (which is unusual) to testify about the huge possibility for success Jonathan possessed. Namely, Jonathan had a close, supportive, extended family, was a good student in school, was well liked by peers, grew up in church and was involved in the youth group, and had goals and plans for his future. Although the DYS person who interviewed Jonathan thought Jonathan would be a good candidate for the program, the DYS worker also said that the judges in our court district typically were difficult to work with and wished Jonathan's case was in a different district. Tragically, the judge in Jonathan's case refused to listen to this recommendation.

Losing Everything

Jonathan left the jail two days later and was placed in several other facilities. On December 13th, Jonathan took his GED test and passed with a 99th percentile in the nation. On January 4th, three days after his 17th birthday he was found hanging in his cell. A few days before, he had learned that he would be going back to Mississippi County to the prison in Charleston, which was the same town where he had lived and witnessed horrible experiences while in the jail.

While in jail, Jonathan lost everything. He lost his freedom, his friends, his safety, his privacy, his sanity, his childhood, skateboarding, swimming, his girlfriend, summer vacation, scholarships, college, dreams, Six Flags, marriages, births, deaths, family vacations, Christmas, Thanksgiving, time with his brother and sister (who now have tattoos in his honor and named their children after him), time with a close extended family and cousins who have always been a huge part of his life, his whole entire future and his life.

Our family also suffered while Jonathan suffered and we nearly lost everything as well. Jonathan's older brother, Charles, had recently moved out on his own, but began experiencing panic attacks and seizures due to extreme stress and worry over Jonathan and was forced to move back home. Shortly after Jonathan died, Charles attempted suicide. A few weeks before Jonathan's death, my husband also attempted suicide and was hospitalized. Jonathan's older sister, Suzanne, who is in the Army National Guard, was scheduled to deploy a few days after Jonathan's death and also ended up in the hospital suffering from panic attacks.

No Child Deserves Such a Fate

Jonathan's experience taught me that no child should be placed with adults no matter what, because when children are put in with adults they die—physically or mentally. I also believe that all kids deserve a second chance. As a parent, one of the most frustrating things for me was that the court, the judges, and the prosecutors didn't know my son—they hadn't raised him like I had; they didn't even know him as a person—but they weren't willing to give him the second chance they might have given to their own kids if they were in the same situation. Finally, if the goal of the juvenile and criminal justice system is to keep our communities safe, how safe can our communities be if a kid in Jonathan's position would have spent five, ten, fifteen or more years in the conditions Jonathan faced and with the role models he had?

> *"Heavy reliance on juvenile incarceration is a counterproductive public policy for combating youth crime."*

Rates of Juvenile Incarceration Should Be Reduced

Richard A. Mendel

In the following viewpoint, a researcher argues that the incarceration of youth offenders is a failed method of rehabilitation and an ineffective means of increasing public safety. The author cites several studies that show recidivism rates are comparatively high for youth who have served time in correctional facilities, and these facilities typically put the offenders at risk of abuse. He maintains young criminals are better served by small treatment facilities that stress individual and family counseling. Thus, he argues that states should adhere to these alternative practices and continue the trend in reducing the number of incarcerated youth. Richard A. Mendel has authored several reports for the Annie E. Casey Foundation, a private charity that seeks to help disadvantaged youth and their families.

A new report, *No Place for Kids: The Case for Reducing Juvenile Incarceration*, published by the Annie E. Casey Foundation, assembles decades of research as well as persuasive new data to demonstrate that America's heavy reliance on juvenile incarceration has not paid off, and in fact, is a failed strategy for combating youth crime.

The latest official national count of youth in custody, conducted in 2007, found that roughly 60,500 U.S. youths were confined in correctional facilities or other residential programs each night on the order of a juvenile delinquency court. The largest share of committed youth—about 40 percent of the total, disproportionately youth of color—are held in locked long-term correctional facilities operated by state governments or private contractors hired by states.

There is compelling evidence that our nation's heavy reliance on youth incarceration:

- Does not reduce future offending by confined youth;
- Provides no overall benefit to public safety;
- Wastes taxpayer dollars; and
- Exposes youth to high levels of violence and abuse.

The report notes that a significant movement away from juvenile incarceration is already underway. Prompted by state budget crises and scandals over abuse in many institutions, more than 50 juvenile corrections facilities have been shut down since 2007 in 18 states. Although these closures signal positive action is being taken, sustainable system improvement will require the mobilization of a coordinated juvenile corrections reform movement.

Youth Incarceration Does Not Rehabilitate

Dozens of recidivism studies from systems across the nation have found that these facilities fail to place youth on the path to success. Re-offending rates for youth released from juvenile correctional facilities are almost uniformly high.

- Within three years of release, around 75 percent of youth are rearrested and 45 to 72 percent are convicted of a new offense.

- In New York State, 89 percent of boys and 81 percent of girls released from state juvenile corrections institutions in the early 1990s were rearrested as adults by age 28.

Nationally, just 12 percent of the nearly 150,000 youth placed into residential programs by delinquency courts in 2007 had committed any of the four most serious violent crimes— aggravated assault, robbery, rape, or homicide. Yet, incarceration has been found to be especially ineffective for less-serious youth offenders.

- In a recent Ohio study, low- and moderate-risk youth placed into correctional facilities were five times more likely to be incarcerated for subsequent offenses than comparable youth placed in community supervision programs.

- In Florida, a 2007 study found that low-risk youth placed into residential facilities not only re-offended at a higher rate than similar youth who remained in the community, they also re-offended at higher rates than high-risk youth placed into correctional facilities.

Finally, research shows that incarceration reduces youths' future success in education and the labor market. One study found that correctional confinement at age 16 or earlier leads to a 26 percent lower chance of graduating high school by age 19. Other studies show that incarceration during adolescence results in substantial and long-lasting reductions in employment.

Reducing Incarceration Does Not Undermine Public Safety

Between 1997 and 2007, the percent of U.S. youth confined in residential facilities declined 24 percent, while the percent incarcerated in long-term secure care correctional institutions plummeted 41 percent. Despite the reduced use of incarceration,

Jerry Riley (left), seventeen, leads a tour of the Northwest Regional Youth Center in Kansas City, Missouri. Treatment-oriented facilities such as this one may be more conducive to rehabilitation than large detention centers. © AP Images/Orlin Wagner.

juvenile crime rates fell across the board from 1997 to 2007, including a 27 percent drop in juvenile arrests for serious violent crimes.

Examining the data in more detail, the report finds no evidence that sharp reductions in juvenile incarceration cause any increase in juvenile crime or violence.

- States that decreased juvenile confinement rates most sharply (40 percent or more) saw a greater decline in juvenile violent crime arrest rates than states that increased their youth confinement rates or decreased them more modestly (less than 40 percent).
- In California, the population in state youth corrections facilities has declined 85 percent since 1996. Yet California's

juvenile crime rates have declined substantially during this period of rapid de-incarceration. In 2009, California's juvenile arrest rate for violent crimes fell to its lowest level since 1970.

Juvenile Incarceration Facilities Waste Taxpayer Dollars

Nationwide, taxpayers spent about $5 billion in 2008 to confine youthful offenders in juvenile institutions.

Most states spend the bulk of their juvenile justice budgets on correctional institutions and other residential placements. According to the American Correctional Association, the average daily cost nationwide to incarcerate one juvenile offender in 2008 was $241. This means that the cost of the average 9 to 12 month stay of one youth is $66,000 to $88,000. This heavy investment in correctional confinement makes little sense given the powerful evidence showing that non-residential programming options deliver equal or better results for a fraction of the cost.

- Florida's Redirection Program provides evidence-based, family-focused treatment as an alternative to residential placements for less-serious youth offenders. Redirection participants are significantly less likely than comparable youth placed in residential facilities to be arrested for a new crime, convicted of a new felony, or sentenced to an adult prison. From 2004 to 2008, the Redirection Program saved $41.6 million through reduced program costs and lower spending to prosecute and punish subsequent crimes.
- The Washington State Institute for Public Policy has estimated that placing one young person in Multi-dimensional Treatment Foster Care, where troubled and delinquent youth live with specially trained foster families while their parents receive counseling and parent training, saves $96,000 in reduced costs to victims and the criminal justice system.

Juvenile Incarceration Facilities Are Often Violent and Abusive Environments

In the past four decades, recurring violence, abuse, and maltreatment have been documented in the publicly funded youth corrections facilities in at least 39 states plus the District of Columbia and Puerto Rico. This disturbing trend is not improving. In 22 of those states (and the District of Columbia) maltreatment has been documented since 2000.

- In 2010, the first national study on sexual abuse in juvenile corrections found that 12 percent of confined youth—more than 3,000 young peoples—reported being victimized sexually by staff or other youth in their facilities.

- A 2008 Associated Press story found that 13,000 claims of abuse had been reported from 2004 through 2007 in state-run juvenile facilities nationwide.

- In the first nationally representative survey of confined youth, published in April 2010, 42 percent said they were somewhat or very afraid of being physically attacked, 45 percent said that staff use force against youth when they don't need to, and 30 percent said that staff place youth in solitary confinement as a form of discipline.

Needed Policy Changes

1. Limit Eligibility for Correctional Placements

States should impose new restrictions that limit incarceration to youth who have committed serious offenses and pose a clear and demonstrable risk to public safety. For instance, Texas enacted a new law in 2007 allowing state correctional commitments only for youth found guilty of felony crimes, and California now permits only youth who have committed violent felonies to be placed in state facilities. Other states have prohibited commitments for low-level offenses except for youth with serious histories of prior offending. Youth should be placed into correctional facilities based only on their crimes committed and risk of re-offense—not on their perceived needs for mental health or behavioral treatment.

2. Invest in Promising Non-Residential Alternatives
States should redirect funds previously spent on incarceration to support a continuum of high-quality treatment and supervision programs. States should give top priority to proven family intervention models, such as Multisystemic Therapy, Functional Family Therapy, and Multi-dimensional Treatment Foster Care, which currently serve only a small fraction of youth who might benefit nationwide. States should also expand access to career preparation and vocational training programs; intensive youth advocate and mentoring programs; and promising models for specialized mental health and substance abuse treatment.

3. Change the Financial Incentives for Incarcerating Youth
States should revamp funding mechanisms to increase the incentives for local courts to treat delinquent youth in their home communities whenever possible. In too many jurisdictions, local juvenile justice officials face a perverse choice between offering youth cost-effective community-based programming (at the expense of local governments) or committing them to more expensive and less effective custody programs (often funded entirely by the states). California, Illinois, Ohio, Pennsylvania, Wisconsin, and Wayne County, Michigan, among others, have adopted funding formulas that increase the incentives for local supervision and treatment.

4. Adopt Best Practice Reforms for Managing Youthful Offenders
States and localities should implement complementary policies and practices that have proven useful for safely reducing the number of youth confined in correctional facilities. States and localities

should limit lengths of stay in correctional facilities and other residential placements, given the research finding that longer periods of incarceration—especially stays over one year—do not reduce future offending, add to state youth corrections budgets, and harm youths' prospects for success in adult life. States should also embrace detention reforms that safely steer many youth away from pre-trial detention centers and reduce the odds they will be placed into correctional facilities. Finally, states should limit correctional placements based on probation rules violations, which account for one in every eight commitments to secure custody.

5. Replace Large Institutions With Small, Treatment-Oriented Facilities for the Dangerous Few

States should place serious and chronic youth offenders into small, humane, and treatment-oriented facilities, such as those operated by Missouri's Division of Youth Services (DYS). Missouri has divided the state into five regions and built a continuum of programs in each. The secure-care facilities house just 30–36 young people. Youth are placed in small groups that participate in education, treatment, meals, and recreation. DYS staff engage the families to help devise successful reentry plans and assign a single case manager to oversee each youth from commitment through release and aftercare, providing extensive supervision and support in the critical reentry period. Through this approach, Missouri's re-offending rates are far lower than other states.

6. Use Data to Hold Youth Corrections Systems Accountable

States should collect more and better information about correctional programs and use the data to hold systems accountable. States must carefully measure re-offense rates of youth released from juvenile correctional facilities, employing rigorous methodologies to track re-offending into early adulthood. States should also monitor youths' progress after release in education, employment, and mental and behavioral health. To minimize the risks of abuse, states should closely monitor conditions of confinement

NUMBER OF YOUTHS HELD IN RESIDENTIAL PLACEMENT FACILITIES IN THE UNITED STATES

MALE

Age	White	Black	Hispanic	American Indian	Asian	Other	Total
12 & younger	225	218	83	11	4	18	559
13	625	666	331	32	13	44	1,711
14	1,685	2,000	1,007	77	39	97	4,905
15	3,314	4,515	2,321	136	90	220	10,596
16	5,021	7,237	3,850	239	153	299	16,799
17	5,487	7,019	4,320	288	237	257	17,608
18 & older	2,916	3,886	2,016	141	98	123	9,180
Total	19,273	25,541	13,928	924	634	1,058	61,358

FEMALE

Age	White	Black	Hispanic	American Indian	Asian	Other	Total
12 & younger	52	58	20	1	0	3	134
13	148	151	41	10	1	17	368
14	350	405	201	51	4	39	1,050
15	756	752	370	45	20	65	2,008
16	1,079	998	482	90	27	65	2,741
17	996	807	409	93	32	45	2,382
18 & older	293	264	139	22	10	23	751
Total	3,674	3,435	1,662	312	94	257	9,434

Taken from: Sickmund, M., Sladky, T.J., Kang, W., and Puzzanchera, C. (2011) "Easy Access to the Census of Juveniles in Residential Placement," Office of Juvenile Justice and Delinquency Prevention, www.ojjdp.gov.

in juvenile facilities, and ensure that all facilities maintain grievance processes that allow confined youth to report mal-treatment and obtain a fair hearing. Finally, given the continuing racial disparities at all levels of our nation's juvenile justice systems, every state and locality should be collecting and analyzing data to identify and correct practices that unfairly impact youth based on their race or ethnicity.

Creating Better Outcomes for Communities and Troubled Youth

The evidence presented in *No Place for Kids* makes clear that heavy reliance on juvenile incarceration is a counterproductive public policy for combating youth crime. It is time to act on this information by abandoning the long-standing incarceration model and embracing a more constructive, humane, and cost-effective approach to youth corrections.

The substantial decreases in reliance on youth prisons over the past decade are significant. However, these reductions have neither been anchored in a strong new national consensus among policy leaders, nor based on comprehensive changes to policy, practice, programming, and financing that will be critical to ensure sustainable, effective alternative responses to juvenile crime.

The Annie E. Casey Foundation hopes that this report can serve as a catalyst for building a new movement for enlightened juvenile corrections reform. If states adopt the recommendations and best practices highlighted in *No Place for Kids* and reallocate funds currently spent on incarceration to more constructive supervision and treatment strategies, there is every reason to believe that the end result will be less crime and more successful futures for America's young people.

> "Not only did the juvenile justice system
> not address my underlying substance
> abuse issue . . . but the experiences I
> had at the center actually made things
> much worse."

A Woman Who Spent Time in a Youth Detention Facility Recounts the Poor Treatment She Received There

Personal Narrative

Rachel Carrión

The author of the following viewpoint describes her placement in a detention program at fifteen because of drug problems and violent behavior. She asserts that instead of helping her with her problems, the detention facility exacerbated them by introducing her to a violent world in which her addiction was exploited. The author argues that the juvenile justice system must be reformed through legislation that will protect other young female offenders from suffering similar injustices. Rachel Carrión is a board member of Community Connections for Youth, a New York–based nonprofit aimed at developing community-based alternatives to incarceration programs for youth.

Rachel Carrión, Testimony, Hearing on "Meeting the Challenges Faced by Girls in the Juvenile Justice System," House Committee on Education and Labor, March 11, 2010.

My experience with the system started when I was 15 years old. I was arrested for the first time when I got into a fight with another girl and was charged with assault. When I was arrested, I was having a rough time in my life—my mother had just passed away and I was very depressed. In order to deal with my depression and loss, I began smoking marijuana to ease the pain I was feeling.

After my arrest, I was first sent to an alternative-to-detention (ATD) program run by Probation. In this program, I had to report every day to a center, which I did. However, I could not stop using drugs and the drug screenings the center did every week kept coming back positive. I needed help addressing my addiction, but instead of providing treatment, the ATD program sent me back to Family Court for violating the conditions of my release. The judge remanded me to a secure juvenile detention center in New York City where I was detained for six months while my court case proceeded. Eventually I was adjudicated a juvenile delinquent and sentenced to 12 months in a placement center in upstate New York, where I was supposed to get help in dealing with my substance abuse issues.

Entering a World of Violence and Exploitation

When I first arrived at the center, I was greeted not by treatment opportunities, but by a culture of violence among my peers and staff members. During my stay, I—like many other young girls in the juvenile justice system—had some horrible experiences, which have left me scarred for life. I saw fights between girls in the facilities, including girls in the facility jumping other girls and fistfights. Some of the fights were so bad that staff had to take girls to the Intensive Care Unit at the local hospital. Staff did nothing to prevent these fights or to help girls feel safe. Staff also regularly used excessive force to keep control in the center. Once, when I wanted to go outside, a staff person grabbed me by the hair and yanked me to the ground for trying to leave without permission.

Other staff would become too friendly with the girls and would even bring in cigarettes, drugs, and other contraband to give or sell to girls in the facility. Some male staff members took advantage of girls as well. After a few months on campus, a male staff member on campus who was in his thirties initiated a sexual relationship with me in exchange for bringing me drugs. In order to meet up, the staff member would arrange for me to leave the campus and pick me up in his car down the road from the facility. He would then transport me off campus to a local hotel. These activities were never documented and or questioned and although the staff member who I had the relationship with was eventually fired, it was only because he screened positive for drugs—not because he was sexually exploiting me.

Climbing up from the Bottom

Because of these experiences in the center, I continued to have a lot of behavioral problems that affected my rehabilitation. Although my family cared a great deal about me, the distance from my home in New York City and the upstate placement center kept them from visiting me, or being meaningfully involved in my reintegration plan. My addiction had never been treated and on my return home, my behavior began to spiral out of control. I started using heavier drugs and then began soliciting my body to support my growing drug habit. It got so bad that I left home and lived on the street, being sexually exploited by adult men in exchange for money or drugs. Eventually I became pregnant with my daughter and I was arrested for prostitution.

Two days after giving birth to my daughter, with my family's help and support, I began my road to recovery by entering two private residential treatment programs: Teen Challenge and Odyssey House. Teen Challenge is a faith-based residential treatment program in Long Island that finally helped me to address my substance abuse issues. It was in Teen Challenge that I found my faith in God and the courage to start over in life. After beginning my treatment at Teen Challenge, I went to Odyssey

Documenting Abuses in the New York Juvenile Justice System

Over the last few years reports, by the Civil Liberties Union and Human Rights Watch, the U.S. Department of Justice and a task force appointed by the governor, have found that a culture of violence pervades New York State's juvenile residential placement centers. A number of investigations have demonstrated that the institutions rely too much on violent restraint, leading to the injury of juveniles, and many of those juveniles are in need of psychological therapy but do not receive it.

Human Rights Watch documented three cases of facility staff having intercourse with young girls. Other reports have cited broken bones and other serious injuries, and in one case a 15-year-old boy from the Bronx was killed at the Tryon Boys Juvenile Rehabilitation Center when two large staff members restrained him.

David King, "'Culture of Violence' Plagues New York's Juvenile Prisons," Gotham Gazette, *January 11, 2010. www.gothamgazette.com.*

House in the Bronx where I completed my treatment, obtained my GED [General Educational Development degree], and received training to become a peer educator and a Home Health Aide. Being in a program close to my family let them visit me frequently, and they were very involved in my treatment. My brother and his wife took custody of my daughter and the Family Court allowed weekly supervised visits with my child with the goal of returning full custody to me if I completed my treatment. In this therapeutic community, I attended constant meetings and support groups, spoke to counselors and to my peers, and received positive feedback. This feedback helped me to learn to retrain my thinking so I know that I struggle with something that may never go away, but that can be maintained as long as I have support and am honest about how I'm feeling and continue to strive to complete my goals I have set for myself.

The System Needs to Protect Youth

My experiences at the juvenile justice facility and the treatment centers could not be more different. Not only did the juvenile justice system not address my underlying substance abuse issue and take me away from my family support system, but the experiences I had at the center actually made things much worse. It was when I came back to my community—close to my family and friends—that I had the support to make a positive change for myself.

By the grace of God, my hard work, and my family's dedication, I am now back on the right track. After completing the program, I got my daughter back and I am now raising her with the help and support of my brother and his wife. I am interested in pursuing a career as a substance abuse counselor to help those who struggle with addiction, and have been accepted as a student at Bronx Community College, where I hope to begin classes in the fall. I am actively involved in the Promised Land Church in the South Bronx where I encourage and support other young women who have been through similar experiences. I also joined Community Connections for Youth, a grassroots non-profit organization that promotes and develops community-based alternatives to incarceration for youth. I serve as a member of the organization's Board of Directors, speaking out on issues faced by youth in the juvenile justice system and making sure the organization's programs meet the needs of the youth it serves.

This Committee [House Committee on Education and Labor] is responsible for working on the Juvenile Justice and Delinquency Prevention Act (JJDPA). Unfortunately, the current JJDPA law does not have anything that protects youth in juvenile justice facilities from the conditions that I faced. I recommend that the Committee include language in the JJDPA to make facilities safer for youth. . . .

In closing, I would like to encourage the Committee to make sure that no other girl has to go through what I did to get the treatment and help that they need.

> *"Juveniles are capable of under-*
> *standing right from wrong and*
> *the consequences of their actions.*
> *Furthermore, they are capable of*
> *forming the requisite intent to kill*
> *to merit the death penalty."*

Juveniles Should Not Be Exempted from the Death Penalty As a Group, but Judged on an Individual Basis

Dan Cutrer

In the following viewpoint, a supporter of the death penalty pro-
vides testimony in the US Supreme Court case Roper v. Simmons
(2005). The author argues that a juvenile murderer deserves the
death penalty if a jury deems the individual sound enough to know
right from wrong. He also contends that the death penalty deters
criminals from killing. The author urges the court to uphold every
state's right to determine which cases merit the death penalty and
which do not. Ultimately, the court found that it is unconstitutional
to impose the death penalty on juveniles under the age of eighteen.
Dan Cutrer is a member of Justice For All Alliance, a pro-victim's
rights organization.

Dan Cutrer, Brief of Amici Curiae Justice for All Alliance in Support of Petitioner, *Roper,*
Superintendent, Potosi Correctional Center v. Simmons, US Supreme Court, 2005.

JFAA [Justice For All Alliance] is an all-volunteer not for profit organization founded in 1993. JFAA's purpose is to support victims of homicide and violent crimes through challenges that they must face on a regular basis, including victim's compensation, community outreach, trial procedures, parole, and clemency hearings. JFAA provides emotional support to victims throughout the process. In addition, JFAA's mission is to act as an advocate for change in the criminal justice system to ensure that the rights of the victims and law-abiding citizens are protected.

Do Not Tread on States' Criminal Jurisdictions

This case [*Roper v. Simmons* (2005)] involves important issues concerning the execution of juveniles that may affect the State of Texas. A decision upholding the Supreme Court of Missouri's ruling would prevent the State of Texas from bringing convicted murderers to justice by properly punishing them under Texas law. This Court has recognized that in punishing criminal offenders, the state plays a role in vindicating the rights of victims. JFAA has an interest in ensuring that the efforts of the State of Texas to vindicate those rights through the administration of its criminal laws are not unduly hampered. JFAA respectfully requests this Court adopt the clear objective criteria defined by this Court evolving from state legislation over the past century as federal law and apply it to the instant case. Furthermore, to ensure that punishment is not disproportionate to the severity of the crime, the Court should focus on the moral culpability of the respondent at the time he committed premeditated murder and embrace the fundamental respect for humanity underlying the Eighth Amendment that requires the Court not group juveniles together as a class but rather acknowledge that they are all different with respect to their experience, maturity, intelligence and moral culpability.

Christopher Simmons was convicted of premeditated murder in the death of Shirley Crook in Missouri in 1993. The appeal of his death sentence reached the US Supreme Court in 2004 and resulted in a landmark Court decision. © AP Images/Missouri Department of Corrections.

Cruel and Unusual Punishment Should Be Determined on a Case-by-Case Basis

The issue before the Court is whether the execution of a person who committed premeditated murder while under the age of eighteen constitutes "cruel and unusual punishment" in violation of the Eighth Amendment to the Constitution of the United States of America.

The Court is using the national standards of decency doctrine in a way that ignores what punishment society really deems acceptable and appropriate because it does not apply the criteria that is reflected through state legislation and defined by the Court as what factors dictate whether punishment is cruel and unusual. The time has come for the Court to adopt as federal law the clear objective criteria it has defined over the past century evolving out of state legislation to determine what punishment constitutes cruel and unusual under the Eighth Amendment. The Court should require all states to apply the criteria on a case-by-case basis focusing on the moral culpability of the defendant.

The foundation of our judicial system is based on moral culpability. In intentional torts and criminal law the judicial system requires a requisite mental state in order to convict one of a crime. In criminal law, specifically murder cases, punishment is imposed according to one's degree of *mens rea* ["guilty mind"]. In fact, one of the rationales for imposing the death penalty—deterrence—is directly linked to one's moral culpability because the threat of death prevents one from forming the intent to kill. The ultimate penalty is imposed on those who intend to kill, understand right from wrong and the consequences of their actions at the time of the act, and nevertheless kill another human being. Juveniles are capable of understanding right from wrong and the consequences of their actions. Furthermore, they are capable of forming the requisite intent to kill to merit the death penalty. They are also capable of being deterred from forming the requisite intent as will be illustrated in the analysis of the instant case.

Juvenile Criminals Must Be Judged on Their Moral Culpability

The Court and a majority of state legislatures have held that individual consideration is a constitutional requirement before sentencing one to death. The Court needs to abide by this requirement and not group juveniles together as a class based on age. Rather, it should recognize that juvenile defendants, even those in the same age group, are shaped by individual life experiences and therefore possess different levels of maturity and make different choices. Consequently, their decisions affect their

The States Had No Consensus on the Juvenile Death Penalty

When *Roper* was decided, there was not an overwhelming national consensus against the juvenile death penalty to conclusively hold it is a cruel and unusual punishment. Twelve states did not allow the death penalty under any circumstances; therefore, they should not have been relevant to any discussion concerning the juvenile death penalty. Of the remaining thirty-eight states that support the death penalty, only eighteen set the minimum age limit for imposing the death penalty at eighteen-years-old. The other twenty death penalty states either set the minimum age at sixteen-years-old, seventeen-years-old, or they did not have an express minimum age. Therefore, fifty-three percent of death penalty states reserved the right to impose the death penalty on a deserving juvenile offender.

> *Julie Rowe, "Mourning the Untimely Death of the Juvenile Death Penalty: An Examination of* Roper v. Simmons *and the Future of the Juvenile Justice System,"* California Western Law Review, *Spring 2006.*

moral responsibility for a crime. . . . To ascertain the issue, a case-by-case analysis is required.

The Court should not focus solely on the states that expressly prohibit the execution of anyone under the age of 18 to decide if there is a national consensus. Rather, the Court should both consider and recognize that there is a national consensus among state legislatures to impose the death penalty on a defendant who did not intend to kill, nor killed, but was a major participant in a felony murder who knew that death was likely to occur.[1] Clearly, this indicates that society deems it acceptable to impose the death penalty on a seventeen-year-old that intended to kill and did in fact kill.

Knowing Right from Wrong

Executing the Respondent [Christopher Simmons] is not cruel and unusual punishment because he specifically knew it was wrong to kill, understood the consequences of his actions, and nevertheless committed a horrific premeditated murder of an innocent woman. His justification for the murder was that he knew his age would prevent him from receiving the ultimate punishment. Juveniles like Simmons need to be deterred from committing such an egregious act for the safety of society by being properly punished. The Respondent's execution furthers the goals of the death penalty because he deserves his life be taken as a result of him intentionally taking an innocent woman's life. Furthermore, it sends a message to other juveniles that when one understands the repercussions, knows right from wrong and still commits premeditated murder, he or she will receive the ultimate penalty.

Note

1. *Tison v. Arizona*, 481 U.S. [1987] at 153–154 (holding that a defendant deserves the death penalty when he is a major participant in a felony murder and acts in a manner that reveals a reckless indifference to human life).

> "It would be misguided to equate the
> failings of a minor with those of an
> adult, for a greater possibility exists
> that a minor's character deficiencies
> will be reformed."

Sentencing a Juvenile Offender to the Death Penalty Violates the Eighth and Fourteenth Amendments

The Supreme Court's Decision

Anthony Kennedy

In the following viewpoint, a US Supreme Court justice argues against imposing the death penalty on juveniles under eighteen. In Atkins v. Virginia (2002), *the court ruled that the Eighth and Fourteenth Amendments prohibit the execution of mentally disabled persons. Building off the* Atkins *verdict, the author claims that executions of minors are declining across the nation, and society is progressing toward abolishing the death penalty for juveniles. He argues that the death penalty is not a deterrent or an appropriate punishment for young people because juveniles are not guided by the same mature reasoning as adults. Anthony Kennedy has served as an associate justice of the Supreme Court since 1988.*

Anthony Kennedy, Majority opinion, *Roper, Superintendent, Potosi Correctional Center v. Simmons*, US Supreme Court, March 1, 2005.

The Eighth Amendment provides: "Excessive bail shall not be required, nor excessive fines imposed, nor cruel and unusual punishments inflicted." The provision is applicable to the States through the Fourteenth Amendment. As the Court explained in *Atkins* [*v. Virginia* (2002)], the Eighth Amendment guarantees individuals the right not to be subjected to excessive sanctions. The right flows from the basic "'precept of justice that punishment for crime should be graduated and proportioned to [the] offense.'" By protecting even those convicted of heinous crimes, the Eighth Amendment reaffirms the duty of the government to respect the dignity of all persons.

Changing Standards of Decency

The prohibition against "cruel and unusual punishments," like other expansive language in the Constitution, must be interpreted according to its text, by considering history, tradition, and precedent, and with due regard for its purpose and function in the constitutional design. To implement this framework we have established the propriety and affirmed the necessity of referring to "the evolving standards of decency that mark the progress of a maturing society" to determine which punishments are so disproportionate as to be cruel and unusual. *Trop v. Dulles* (1958).

In *Thompson v. Oklahoma* (1988), a plurality of the Court determined that our standards of decency do not permit the execution of any offender under the age of 16 at the time of the crime. The plurality opinion explained that no death penalty State that had given express consideration to a minimum age for the death penalty had set the age lower than 16. The plurality also observed that "[t]he conclusion that it would offend civilized standards of decency to execute a person who was less than 16 years old at the time of his or her offense is consistent with the views that have been expressed by respected professional organizations, by other nations that share our Anglo-American heritage, and by the leading members of the Western European community." The opinion further noted that juries imposed the death penalty on offenders under 16 with exceeding rarity; the last execution of an offender for a crime committed under the age of 16 had been carried out in 1948, 40 years prior.

Bringing its independent judgment to bear on the permissibility of the death penalty for a 15-year-old offender, the *Thompson* plurality stressed that "[t]he reasons why juveniles are not trusted with the privileges and responsibilities of an adult also explain why their irresponsible conduct is not as morally reprehensible as that of an adult." According to the plurality, the lesser culpability of offenders under 16 made the death penalty inappropriate as a form of retribution, while the low likelihood that offenders under 16 engaged in "the kind of cost-benefit analysis that attaches any weight to the possibility of execution" made the death penalty ineffective as a means of deterrence.

The next year, in *Stanford v. Kentucky* (1989), the Court, over a dissenting opinion joined by four Justices, referred to contemporary standards of decency in this country and concluded the Eighth and Fourteenth Amendments did not proscribe the execution of juvenile offenders over 15 but under 18. The Court noted that 22 of the 37 death penalty States permitted the death penalty for 16-year-old offenders, and, among these 37 States, 25 permitted it for 17-year-old offenders. These numbers, in the Court's view, indicated there was no national consensus "sufficient to label a particular punishment cruel and unusual." A plurality of the Court also "emphatically reject[ed]" the suggestion that the Court should bring its own judgment to bear on the acceptability of the juvenile death penalty.

The same day the Court decided *Stanford*, it held that the Eighth Amendment did not mandate a categorical exemption from the death penalty for the mentally retarded. *Penry v. Lynaugh* (1989). In reaching this conclusion it stressed that only two States had enacted laws banning the imposition of the death penalty on a mentally retarded person convicted of a capital offense. According to the Court, "the two state statutes

NATIONAL CONSENSUS ON THE JUVENILE DEATH PENALTY

No Death Penalty	No Death Penalty for Juveniles	No Juvenile Offenders Executed Since 1976	No Juvenile Offenders On Death Row
12 States	31 States	43 States	38 States
Alaska	California	*Exceptions:*	*Exceptions:*
Hawaii	Colorado	Georgia	Alabama
Iowa	Connecticut	Louisiana	Arizona
Maine	Illinois	Missouri (now	Florida
Massachusetts	Indiana	banned)	Georgia
Michigan	Kansas	Oklahoma	Louisiana
Minnesota	Maryland	South Carolina	Mississippi
North Dakota	Missouri	Texas	Nevada
Rhode Island	Montana	Virginia	North Carolina
Vermont	Nebraska		Pennsylvania
West Virginia	New Jersey		South Carolina
Wisconsin	New Mexico		Texas
	New York		Virginia
Also:	Ohio		
Puerto Rico	Oregon		
Washington, DC	South Dakota		
	Tennessee		
	Washington		
	Wyoming		
	Also:		
	US federal government		
	US military		

Taken from: Mary Madden and Amanda Lenhart, "Teens and Distracted Driving," Pew Research Center, November 16, 2009. www.pewinternet.org.

prohibiting execution of the mentally retarded, even when added to the 14 States that have rejected capital punishment completely, [did] not provide sufficient evidence at present of a national consensus."

Atkins v. Virginia Revealed a National Consensus on Excessive Punishment

Three Terms ago the subject was reconsidered in *Atkins*. We held that standards of decency have evolved since *Penry* and now demonstrate that the execution of the mentally retarded is cruel and unusual punishment. The Court noted objective indicia [signs and circumstances] of society's standards, as expressed in legislative enactments and state practice with respect to executions of the mentally retarded. When *Atkins* was decided only a minority of States permitted the practice, and even in those States it was rare. On the basis of these indicia the Court determined that executing mentally retarded offenders "has become truly unusual, and it is fair to say that a national consensus has developed against it."

The inquiry into our society's evolving standards of decency did not end there. The *Atkins* Court neither repeated nor relied upon the statement in *Stanford* that the Court's independent judgment has no bearing on the acceptability of a particular punishment under the Eighth Amendment. Instead we returned to the rule, established in decisions predating *Stanford*, that "'the Constitution contemplates that in the end our own judgment will be brought to bear on the question of the acceptability of the death penalty under the Eighth Amendment.'" Mental retardation, the Court said, diminishes personal culpability even if the offender can distinguish right from wrong. The impairments of mentally retarded offenders make it less defensible to impose the death penalty as retribution for past crimes and less likely that the death penalty will have a real deterrent effect. . . .

Juvenile Death Sentences Are Infrequent

The evidence of national consensus against the death penalty for juveniles is similar, and in some respects parallel, to the evidence *Atkins* held sufficient to demonstrate a national consensus against the death penalty for the mentally retarded. When *Atkins* was decided, 30 States prohibited the death penalty for the mentally retarded. This number comprised 12 that had abandoned the death penalty altogether, and 18 that maintained it but excluded the mentally retarded from its reach. By a similar calculation in this case, 30 States prohibit the juvenile death penalty, comprising 12 that have rejected the death penalty altogether and 18 that maintain it but, by express provision or judicial interpretation, exclude juveniles from its reach. *Atkins* emphasized that even in the 20 States without formal prohibition, the practice of executing the mentally retarded was infrequent. Since *Penry*, only five States had executed offenders known to have an IQ under 70. In the present case, too, even in the 20 States without a formal prohibition on executing juveniles, the practice is infrequent. Since *Stanford*, six States have executed prisoners for crimes committed as juveniles. In the past 10 years, only three have done so: Oklahoma, Texas, and Virginia. . . .

A Clear Trend Toward National Abolition of the Juvenile Death Penalty

Though less dramatic than the change from *Penry* to *Atkins*, we still consider the change from *Stanford* to this case to be significant. As noted in *Atkins*, with respect to the States that had abandoned the death penalty for the mentally retarded since *Penry*, "[i]t is not so much the number of these States that is significant, but the consistency of the direction of change." In particular we found it significant that, in the wake of *Penry*, no State that had already prohibited the execution of the mentally retarded had passed legislation to reinstate the penalty. The

People line up outside the US Supreme Court building in Washington, DC, on October 13, 2004, to hear arguments in Roper v. Simmons. © AP Images/Manuel Balce Ceneta.

number of States that have abandoned capital punishment for juvenile offenders since *Stanford* is smaller than the number of States that abandoned capital punishment for the mentally retarded after *Penry;* yet we think the same consistency of direction of change has been demonstrated. Since *Stanford*, no State that previously prohibited capital punishment for juveniles has reinstated it. . . .

As in *Atkins*, the objective indicia of consensus in this case—the rejection of the juvenile death penalty in the majority of States; the infrequency of its use even where it remains on the books; and the consistency in the trend toward abolition of the practice—provide sufficient evidence that today our society views juveniles, in the words *Atkins* used respecting the mentally retarded, as "categorically less culpable than the average criminal."

Juveniles Cannot Be Classified Among the Worst Offenders

A majority of States have rejected the imposition of the death penalty on juvenile offenders under 18, and we now hold this is required by the Eighth Amendment.

Because the death penalty is the most severe punishment, the Eighth Amendment applies to it with special force. Capital punishment must be limited to those offenders who commit "a narrow category of the most serious crimes" and whose extreme culpability makes them "the most deserving of execution." *Atkins.* This principle is implemented throughout the capital sentencing process. States must give narrow and precise definition to the aggravating factors that can result in a capital sentence. In any capital case a defendant has wide latitude to raise as a mitigating factor "any aspect of [his or her] character or record and any of the circumstances of the offense that the defendant proffers as a basis for a sentence less than death." *Lockett v. Ohio* (1978). . . .

Three general differences between juveniles under 18 and adults demonstrate that juvenile offenders cannot with reliability be classified among the worst offenders. First, as any parent knows and as the scientific and sociological studies respondent and his *amici* [an expert testimony volunteered in court] cite tend to confirm, "[a] lack of maturity and an underdeveloped sense of responsibility are found in youth more often than in adults and are more understandable among the young. These qualities often result in impetuous and ill-considered actions and decisions." *Johnson* [*v. Texas* (1993)]. . . .

The second area of difference is that juveniles are more vulnerable or susceptible to negative influences and outside pressures, including peer pressure. . . .

The third broad difference is that the character of a juvenile is not as well formed as that of an adult. The personality traits of juveniles are more transitory, less fixed.

These differences render suspect any conclusion that a juvenile falls among the worst offenders. The susceptibility of juveniles to immature and irresponsible behavior means "their irresponsible conduct is not as morally reprehensible as that of an adult." *Thompson*. Their own vulnerability and comparative lack of control over their immediate surroundings mean juveniles have a greater claim than adults to be forgiven for failing to escape negative influences in their whole environment. . . . The reality that juveniles still struggle to define their identity means it is less supportable to conclude that even a heinous crime committed by a juvenile is evidence of irretrievably depraved character. From a moral standpoint it would be misguided to equate the failings of a minor with those of an adult, for a greater possibility exists that a minor's character deficiencies will be reformed. . . .

In *Thompson*, a plurality of the Court recognized the import of these characteristics with respect to juveniles under 16, and relied on them to hold that the Eighth Amendment prohibited the imposition of the death penalty on juveniles below that age. We conclude the same reasoning applies to all juvenile offenders under 18.

> "No national trend exists moving away
> from harsh sentences for serious crimes
> such as rape; in fact, a nationwide
> trend of getting tougher on crime has
> occurred."

Minors Should Be Sentenced to Life in Prison Without Parole Under Certain Circumstances

Scott D. Makar

In the following viewpoint, the solicitor general of Florida offers a testimonial to the US Supreme Court in the 2009 case of Sullivan v. Florida. *He maintains that many states have imposed life sentences without parole for juvenile offenders. The author contends that state judiciaries consider age in trial and sentencing procedures, but juveniles should be punished based on the severity of their crimes. He encourages the court to refrain from undermining the power of the states in administering justice. Scott D. Makar has served as the solicitor general of Florida since 2007.*

The Eighth Amendment contains no textual or jurispruden-
tial basis for a categorical ban on life sentences without pa-

role for juveniles of a certain age who commit heinous, violent crimes against vulnerable victims, as Joe Harris Sullivan did. He completely ignores [the US Supreme Court's] narrow proportionality jurisprudence as it applies to prison term sentences.

This Court has repeatedly held that a sentence of a term of years violates the Eighth Amendment only in "exceedingly rare" cases in which an inference of "gross disproportionality" can be drawn. No inference of gross disproportionality exists for a life sentence arising from the brutal crime of sexual battery, particularly given this Court's characterization of rape as an especially heinous crime, second only to murder. Moreover, this Court has never factored in age in the gross disproportionality analysis, and should not do so in considering particularly violent adult crimes, such as rape. . . .

Admittedly, the number of juveniles who received these sentences is fewer as the age of the offender declines; but that fact does not undermine the societal consensus that juveniles of even Sullivan's age may be treated as adults in the criminal justice system. Indeed, other courts have affirmed life sentences for juveniles for the especially heinous crime of sexual battery. No national trend exists moving away from harsh sentences for serious crimes such as rape; in fact, a nationwide trend of getting tougher on crime has occurred over the last two decades since Sullivan was sentenced. Given this national trend, no basis exists for this Court to make comparisons with international law. Even when national comparisons are made, Sullivan cannot show that the sentence for the violent crimes he committed was grossly disproportional. . . .

Sullivan's Punishment Was Just

As a threshold matter, Sullivan's life sentence is not grossly disproportionate to the violent and brutal sexual batteries he committed against the 72-year-old victim, particularly when compared to the cases in which this Court has upheld similar sentences for lesser, nonviolent property crimes.

In a controversial 1993 case, Chris Thrasher was convicted of murder at age sixteen in Alabama and sentenced to life in prison. The initials of the victims, who were his friends, are tattooed on his arms. © Andrew Lichtenstein/Corbis.

In five of its six cases involving proportionality review of prison terms, this Court affirmed lengthy, oftentimes mandatory sentences, many of them for life terms: (a) a mandatory life sentence (with the possibility of parole) for three theft-related felonies (under a recidivist statute), which, in the aggregate, totaled less than $230, *Rummel v. Estelle* (1980); (b) a 40-year sentence for possession and distribution of less than 9 ounces of marijuana, *Hutto v. Davis* (1982); (c) a mandatory life sentence (without the possibility of parole) for possession of 672 grams of cocaine, *Harmelin v. Michigan* (1991); (d) a 25-year-to-life sentence pursuant to California's mandatory Three Strikes law where the triggering offense was felony grand theft of three golf clubs amounting to approximately $1,200, *Ewing v. California* (2003); and (e) two consecutive 25-year-to-life sentences under

California's mandatory Three Strikes law for two counts of petty theft of videocassettes valued at approximately $150, *Lockyer* [*v. Andrade* (2003)].

The only instance where this Court struck down a prison sentence as unconstitutional was a mandatory life sentence without parole for a seventh nonviolent felony, the last being a $100 bad check charge. In *Solem v. Helm* (1983), as in all cases involving an application of the narrow "gross disproportionality" standard, the Court has found no constitutional violation if, at the threshold, the seriousness of the offense when compared with the sentence given does not raise an inference of gross disproportionality. An offense's gravity, including the measure of the harm caused to the victim and the violent nature of the crime, are considered. Heretofore, the Court has considered nothing more.

Sullivan's brutal rape of an elderly woman in her own home qualifies as one of the most serious and violent crimes in our society, and is everywhere acknowledged to be one that inflicts serious physical and emotional harm to the victim. Sullivan's life sentence for the two violent sexual battery counts is not a grossly disproportionate sentence under this Court's precedents. If a mandatory life sentence without parole for the mere passive possession of 672 grams of cocaine is constitutional, *Harmelin*, and a mandatory life sentence with the possibility of parole for three theft-related felonies is constitutional, *Rummel*, then it logically follows that a similar sentence for a violent sexual battery is not grossly disproportionate. . . .

Although the Court has not considered age (or any other individual characteristic) in the gross disproportionality analysis, in this case it raises no inference of a constitutional violation. Here, Sullivan's crime was so serious that an inference can be drawn that he intended to commit these heinous acts with knowledge of their seriousness. Some crimes, such as murder and rape, can be sufficiently horrific that a State's criminal justice system, as formulated by its legislature and implemented by its trial courts, can conclude that a juvenile offender was sufficiently mature to commit those crimes with adult intent. As such, Sullivan—even if he attempted to do so—does not survive the initial threshold, ending the constitutional analysis at this point.

Life Sentences Are Not Rare in State Judiciary Systems

Because Sullivan's sentence is not grossly disproportionate, it is unnecessary to consider intra- and interjurisdictional analyses, which "are appropriate only in the rare case in which a threshold comparison of the crime committed and the sentence available leads to an inference of gross disproportionality."—*Harmelin*. Sullivan, however, argues that considering his age at the time of the crimes, the imposition of a life sentence is a "freakishly rare" occurrence in most States.

Sullivan does not explicitly engage in the type of jurisdictional analysis this Court has traditionally considered in its non-capital cases. Instead, citing only the Court's death penalty precedents, he claims that "objective *indicia*" [evidence] show a national consensus exists against ever imposing a life sentence without parole upon young juveniles regardless of their offense. Neither a proper jurisdictional analysis nor Sullivan's "objective factors" support a constitutional violation.

Moreover, even if this Court were to deem it necessary to proceed to the second step of the "gross disproportionality" analysis and conduct an interjurisdictional analysis of the States, it would find that all States consider age as a crucial factor throughout their criminal justice systems, from separate juvenile systems to decisions regarding adult charges and sentences. Such an analysis provides no justification for the age-based categorical Eighth Amendment rule Sullivan is seeking.

First, turning to intrajurisdictional analysis, life sentences without parole may be imposed in Florida for all life and many first-degree felonies, which involve a wide variety of crimes. Juveniles may be tried as adults for these crimes, and if convicted, can be subject to the same sentences as adults. These categories of felonies are comparable to Sullivan's sexual battery, a number being less violent than a sexual battery. As such, life sentences may be imposed on juveniles who commit crimes of both greater and lesser violence in Florida.

As to actual sentencing data, the Florida Department of Corrections reports that the number of persons serving life sentences for sexual battery in Florida is 478. Moreover, out of 301 juvenile offenders currently serving life sentences in Florida, more than half were sentenced for a nonhomicide offense—including dozens for offenses less violent than Sullivan's. Thirty-nine juveniles were given life sentences for sexual battery. Thus, life sentences are both theoretically available and actually imposed in Florida, and are not isolated or rare events. Sullivan's claim that this type of sentence is rare in Florida cannot be sustained.

Turning to interjurisdictional comparisons, Florida's sentencing laws and rates are not out of line with national data, especially given its comparatively higher population (nearly 19 million) and juvenile crime problem. A supermajority of States—42—permits the imposition of life without parole on a juvenile. Of those, 38 States permit that sentence for crimes other than those resulting in the death of a victim. Notably, Sullivan's concession that at least 40 States allow life without parole for 14-year-olds, 27 of which allow it for 13-year-olds, is telling. Sullivan characterizes this potential as "broad theoretical availability," thus conceding that the "sentence available" for the crime he committed at age thirteen would be life without parole in 27 of the 50 States. This data reflects consensus rather than condemnation, more so given no contrary trend exists.

Courts nationwide have sentenced violent offenders to life for similar sexual battery crimes. In addition, a 2005 *New York Times* study found that more than 25,000 offenders are serving life for nonhomicide crimes like rape, kidnapping, armed robbery, assault, extortion, burglary, and arson (16 percent of lifers were convicted of drug trafficking). Even with such a large number of life-sentenced inmates for nonhomicide crimes, however, there is no available data on the number of juveniles nationwide serving a life sentence for the crime of rape.

Life without parole is within the mainstream of State sentencing practices for his crime. No clear national trend indicates that States are moving away from life without parole sentences for juveniles. Indeed, one study (by a group opposed to juvenile life without parole) reports that nationally the number of juvenile offenders serving life sentences in the last 25 years has more than quadrupled, with large States such as Pennsylvania, California, and Michigan accounting for the most juveniles serving life without parole sentences. . . .

Sentencing Accounts for the Age of the Offender

The medical and social science research on juvenile development upon which Sullivan heavily relies for his constitutional argument does little to advance his position. In fact, the States have recognized the differences between juveniles and adults by treating the two differently within their criminal justice systems, unless a decision is made that under the circumstances, a juvenile should be treated as an adult. As noted, Sullivan does not challenge these decisions, nor does he challenge the longstanding systems all 50 States already have in place to account for youth in the administration of criminal justice.

It has been well known for ages that juveniles generally lack mature judgment and that their age level matters in many contexts. In fact, Sullivan points to "hundreds" of State and Federal laws that, in various contexts, recognize the special nature of juveniles and afford them differential treatment. Yet Sullivan omits from this extensive list the wide swath of laws nationwide and in Florida that give special consideration to juveniles in the criminal justice system.

All States have laws establishing juvenile justice systems and programs to contend with the vast majority of youthful offenders.

Juvenile Murderers Should Not Be Termed "Children"

Advocates who continually call [juvenile life without parole offenders] "children" need to consider the impact of this argument on the victims of these crimes, not just use it for its propaganda impact on the public, and publishing pictures of the offenders (as they have many times) when they were much younger than when they actually committed the crimes. Calling these murderers "children" constantly in their advocacy work is incredibly emotionally troubling to many victims' families—some have described it to us as a dagger into them each time the offender is called that. It is worst when the actual murder victim was a real child. Many of these cases were 17 year olds killing, for example, 5 year olds. To hear the offenders called "children" all the time to the mother of a murdered young girl is beyond painful.

"Children" is not a term teens themselves would accept. Those who use this term to describe these offenders are only using it for one purpose—to paint an inaccurate picture of the crimes to propagandize for support for the offenders.

Jennifer Bishop-Jenkins, National Organization of Victims of Juvenile Lifers, Testimony to the United States Congress Re: HR2289, The Juvenile Justice and Accountability Act of 2009, June 9, 2009. http://judiciary.house.gov.

These systems deal with juvenile crime problems ranging from the minor types of youthful indiscretions that occur with regularity to the less frequent, but horrific premeditated acts of violence. That society may assign lesser culpability to juveniles as a class does not compel the conclusion that states may not punish as adults those who intentionally cause serious harm and violence to others.

Indeed, Sullivan's argument reduces to the unacceptable proposition that because juveniles as a class lack full maturity and judgment, none—even those who plan and commit the most heinous acts—can be constitutionally punished with lengthy sentences. But States have overwhelmingly decided that those juveniles who engage in certain types of "adult" crimes that involve the planning and premeditation of acts of violence may be treated differently. To do so does not ignore that many juvenile acts are not suitable for "adult" treatment; indeed, the data overwhelmingly show that society generally treats most juveniles as a class with great lenience when compared to adults.

Sullivan does not contend that he was not properly indicted as an adult; rather, he only challenges the end result, an adult sentence that he claims cannot be applied to any juveniles of a certain age adjudicated as adults. His reasoning is circular. A major reason for the laws allowing the filing of "adult" charges against juveniles is to provide for potentially stiffer "adult" sanctions to deter and punish, a feature of State direct-file systems that would be undermined radically if age categorically bars harsher punishments. This Court should not create a categorical Eighth Amendment rule that upsets the balance States have struck between adjudicating juveniles in their juvenile justice systems and adjudicating some juveniles of exceptionally serious crimes as adult in the adult systems.

> "A juvenile offender will on average
> serve more years and a greater
> percentage of his life in prison than
> an adult offender."

It Is Unconstitutional to Sentence Minors to Life in Prison Without Parole for Crimes Less than Homicide

The Supreme Court's Decision

Anthony Kennedy

In the following viewpoint, a US Supreme Court justice maintains that life imprisonment without the possibility of parole is a cruel and unusual punishment for juveniles who commit nonhomicide crimes. The author argues that young offenders are not as culpable as adult offenders, and they possess a greater capacity to reform. He contends that states must provide an opportunity for juveniles to obtain release based on evidence of demonstrated maturity and rehabilitation. Anthony Kennedy has served as an associate justice of the Supreme Court since 1988.

Anthony Kennedy, Majority opinion, *Terrance Jamar Graham, Petitioner v. Florida*, US Supreme Court, May 17, 2010.

The Eighth Amendment states: "Excessive bail shall not be required, nor excessive fines imposed, nor cruel and unusual punishments inflicted." To determine whether a punishment is cruel and unusual, courts must look beyond historical conceptions to "'the evolving standards of decency that mark the progress of a maturing society.'" *Estelle v. Gamble* (1976). "This is because '[t]he standard of extreme cruelty is not merely descriptive, but necessarily embodies a moral judgment. The standard itself remains the same, but its applicability must change as the basic mores of society change.'" *Kennedy v. Louisiana* (2008). . . .

Defining Cruel and Unusual Punishment

For the most part, however, the [US Supreme] Court's precedents consider punishments challenged not as inherently barbaric but as disproportionate to the crime. The concept of proportionality is central to the Eighth Amendment. Embodied in the Constitution's ban on cruel and unusual punishments is the "precept of justice that punishment for crime should be graduated and proportioned to [the] offense." *Weems v. United States* (1910).

The Court's cases addressing the proportionality of sentences fall within two general classifications. The first involves challenges to the length of term-of-years sentences given all the circumstances in a particular case. The second comprises cases in which the Court implements the proportionality standard by certain categorical restrictions on the death penalty.

In the first classification the Court considers all of the circumstances of the case to determine whether the sentence is unconstitutionally excessive. Under this approach, the Court has held unconstitutional a life without parole sentence for the defendant's seventh nonviolent felony, the crime of passing a worthless check. *Solem v. Helm* (1983). In other cases, however, it has been difficult for the challenger to establish a lack of proportionality. A leading case is *Harmelin v. Michigan*, (1991), in which the offender was sentenced under state law to life without parole for possessing a large quantity of cocaine. A closely divided Court upheld the sentence. The controlling opinion concluded that the Eighth Amendment contains a "narrow proportionality principle," that "does not require strict proportionality between crime and sentence" but rather "forbids only extreme sentences that are 'grossly disproportionate' to the crime." . . .

The controlling opinion in *Harmelin* explained its approach for determining whether a sentence for a term of years is grossly disproportionate for a particular defendant's crime. A court must begin by comparing the gravity of the offense and the severity of the sentence. "[I]n the rare case in which [this] threshold comparison . . . leads to an inference of gross disproportionality" the court should then compare the defendant's sentence with the sentences received by other offenders in the same jurisdiction and with the sentences imposed for the same crime in other jurisdictions. If this comparative analysis "validate[s] an initial judgment that [the] sentence is grossly disproportionate," the sentence is cruel and unusual. . . .

A National Trend to Restrict Harsh Punishments

The analysis begins with objective indicia [signs and circumstances] of national consensus. "[T]he 'clearest and most reliable objective evidence of contemporary values is the legislation enacted by the country's legislatures'" *Atkins* [*v. Virginia* (2002)]. . . . Six jurisdictions do not allow life without parole sentences for any juvenile offenders. Seven jurisdictions permit life without parole for juvenile offenders, but only for homicide crimes. Thirty-seven States as well as the District of Columbia permit sentences of life without parole for a juvenile nonhomicide offender in some circumstances. Federal law also allows for the possibility of life without parole for offenders as young as 13. Relying on this metric, the State and its *amici* [experts who volunteer testimony] argue that there is no national consensus against the sentencing practice at issue. . . .

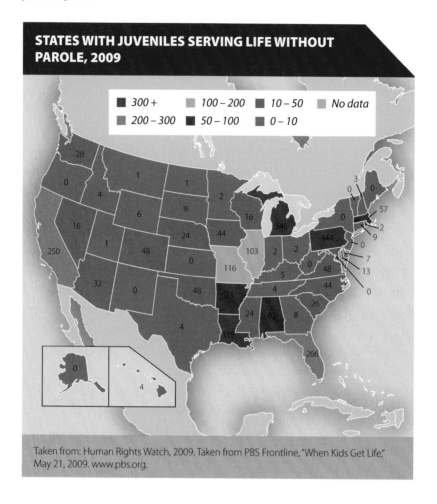

STATES WITH JUVENILES SERVING LIFE WITHOUT PAROLE, 2009

Legend: ■ 300+ ■ 100–200 ■ 10–50 ■ No data
■ 200–300 ■ 50–100 ■ 0–10

Taken from: Human Rights Watch, 2009. Taken from PBS Frontline, "When Kids Get Life," May 21, 2009. www.pbs.org.

Actual sentencing practices are an important part of the Court's inquiry into consensus. Here, an examination of actual sentencing practices in jurisdictions where the sentence in question is permitted by statute discloses a consensus against its use. Although these statutory schemes contain no explicit prohibition on sentences of life without parole for juvenile nonhomicide offenders, those sentences are most infrequent. According to a recent study, nationwide there are only 109 juvenile offenders serving sentences of life without parole for nonhomicide offenses. . . .

The States Have No Consensus on Harsh Punishments for Juveniles

The evidence of consensus is not undermined by the fact that many jurisdictions do not prohibit life without parole for juvenile nonhomicide offenders. The Court confronted a similar situation in *Thompson*, where a plurality concluded that the death penalty for offenders younger than 16 was unconstitutional. A number of States then allowed the juvenile death penalty if one considered the statutory scheme. As is the case here, those States authorized the transfer of some juvenile offenders to adult court; and at that point there was no statutory differentiation between adults and juveniles with respect to authorized penalties. The plurality concluded that the transfer laws show "that the States consider 15-year-olds to be old enough to be tried in criminal court for serious crimes (or too old to be dealt with effectively in juvenile court), *but tells us nothing about the judgment these States have made regarding the appropriate punishment for such youthful offenders.*" . . .

The same reasoning obtains here. Many States have chosen to move away from juvenile court systems and to allow juveniles to be transferred to, or charged directly in, adult court, under certain circumstances. Once in adult court, a juvenile offender may receive the same sentence as would be given to an adult offender, including a life without parole sentence. But the fact that transfer and direct charging laws make life without parole possible for some juvenile nonhomicide offenders does not justify a judgment that many States intended to subject such offenders to life without parole sentences.

For example, under Florida law a child of any age can be prosecuted as an adult for certain crimes and can be sentenced to life without parole. The State acknowledged at oral argument that even a 5-year-old, theoretically, could receive such a sentence under the letter of the law. All would concede this to be unrealistic, but the example underscores that the statutory eligibility of a juvenile offender for life without parole does not indicate that the penalty has been endorsed through deliberate, express, and full legislative consideration. Similarly, the many States that allow life without parole for juvenile nonhomicide offenders but do not impose the punishment should not be treated as if they have expressed the view that the sentence is appropriate. The sentencing practice now under consideration is exceedingly rare. And "it is fair to say that a national consensus has developed against it." *Atkins.* . . .

Cases That Suggest Leniency Toward Juvenile Offenders

Roper established that because juveniles have lessened culpability they are less deserving of the most severe punishments. As compared to adults, juveniles have a "'lack of maturity and an underdeveloped sense of responsibility'"; they "are more vulnerable or susceptible to negative influences and outside pressures, including peer pressure"; and their characters are "not as well formed." These salient characteristics mean that "[i]t is difficult even for expert psychologists to differentiate between the juvenile offender whose crime reflects unfortunate yet transient immaturity, and the rare juvenile offender whose crime reflects irreparable corruption." Accordingly, "juvenile offenders cannot with reliability be classified among the worst offenders." A juvenile is not absolved of responsibility for his actions, but his transgression "is not as morally reprehensible as that of an adult." *Thompson.*

No recent data provide reason to reconsider the Court's observations in *Roper* about the nature of juveniles. As petitioner's *amici* point out, developments in psychology and brain science continue to show fundamental differences between juvenile and adult minds. For example, parts of the brain involved in behavior control continue to mature through late adolescence. Juveniles are more capable of change than are adults, and their actions are less likely to be evidence of "irretrievably depraved character" than are the actions of adults. *Roper.* It remains true that "[f]rom a moral standpoint it would be misguided to equate the failings of a minor with those of an adult, for a greater possibility exists that a minor's character deficiencies will be reformed." *Roper.* These matters relate to the status of the offenders in question; and it is relevant to consider next the nature of the offenses to which this harsh penalty might apply.

Nonhomicide Crimes Are Less Deserving of Harsh Punishment

The Court has recognized that defendants who do not kill, intend to kill, or foresee that life will be taken are categorically less deserving of the most serious forms of punishment than are murderers. There is a line "between homicide and other serious violent offenses against the individual." *Kennedy.* Serious nonhomicide crimes "may be devastating in their harm . . . but 'in terms of moral depravity and of the injury to the person and to the public,' . . . they cannot be compared to murder in their 'severity and irrevocability.'" This is because "[l]ife is over for the victim of the murderer," but for the victim of even a very serious nonhomicide crime, "life . . . is not over and normally is not beyond repair." Although an offense like robbery or rape is "a serious crime deserving serious punishment," *Enmund* [*v. Florida* (1982)], those crimes differ from homicide crimes in a moral sense.

It follows that, when compared to an adult murderer, a juvenile offender who did not kill or intend to kill has a twice diminished moral culpability. The age of the offender and the nature of the crime each bear on the analysis.

As for the punishment, life without parole is "the second most severe penalty permitted by law." *Harmelin.* It is true that a death sentence is "unique in its severity and irrevocability," *Gregg v. Georgia* (1976); yet life without parole sentences share some characteristics with death sentences that are shared by no other sentences. The State does not execute the offender sentenced to life without parole, but the sentence alters the offender's life by a forfeiture that is irrevocable. It deprives the convict of the most basic liberties without giving hope of restoration, except perhaps by executive clemency—the remote possibility of which does not mitigate the harshness of the sentence. As one court observed in overturning a life without parole sentence for a juvenile defendant, this sentence "means denial of hope; it means that good behavior and character improvement are immaterial; it means that whatever the future might hold in store for the mind and spirit of [the convict], he will remain in prison for the rest of his days." *Naovarath v. State* (1989). . . .

Life without parole is an especially harsh punishment for a juvenile. Under this sentence a juvenile offender will on average serve more years and a greater percentage of his life in prison than an adult offender. A 16-year-old and a 75-year-old each sentenced to life without parole receive the same punishment in name only. . . .

Life Without Parole Is Not Justifiable for Nonhomicide Crimes Committed by Juveniles

Retribution is a legitimate reason to punish, but it cannot support the sentence at issue here. Society is entitled to impose severe sanctions on a juvenile nonhomicide offender to express its condemnation of the crime and to seek restoration of the moral imbalance caused by the offense. But "[t]he heart of the retribution rationale is that a criminal sentence must be directly related to the personal culpability of the criminal offender." *Tison* [*v. Arizona* (1987)]. And as *Roper* observed, "[w]hether viewed as an attempt to express the community's moral outrage or as an attempt to right the balance for the wrong to the victim, the case for retribution is not as strong with a minor as with an adult." The case becomes even weaker with respect to a juvenile who did not commit homicide. . . .

In sum, penological theory is not adequate to justify life without parole for juvenile nonhomicide offenders. This determination; the limited culpability of juvenile nonhomicide offenders;

Dominic Culpepper was sentenced to life in prison without parole at age fourteen for beating a neighbor to death in a fight. The Graham v. Florida Supreme Court *decision establishes that life imprisonment is allowed in murder convictions such as his.* © Andrew Lichtenstein/ Corbis.

and the severity of life without parole sentences all lead to the conclusion that the sentencing practice under consideration is cruel and unusual. This Court now holds that for a juvenile offender who did not commit homicide the Eighth Amendment forbids the sentence of life without parole. This clear line is necessary to prevent the possibility that life without parole sentences will be imposed on juvenile nonhomicide offenders who are not sufficiently culpable to merit that punishment.

> "I came to realize that I am the only person that is responsible for my actions, and for all the choices that I make in my life."

A Prisoner Explains How He Has Grown to Understand the Significance of His Crime

Personal Narrative

James Earl Jackson

In the following viewpoint, an inmate in a Wisconsin prison explains how growing up without a mother or father led him to act impulsively and without regard to consequences. When he was sixteen years old, he shot a man, turned himself in for the crime, and was handed a sentence of life imprisonment. Now, the author contends that maturing behind bars has given him the time to think about the seriousness of his crime and to work at changing his life for the better. James Earl Jackson hopes to earn parole and help alter the paths of other troubled youth.

My name is James Earl Jackson. I was born in St. Louis, MO, on April 1, 1976. I am now 36 years old. I am the second oldest of four. I am my mother's only son.

I grew up on the north side of Milwaukee. My mother moved here after my father was killed in St. Louis. My father was shot and killed just two weeks after my second birthday. I was too young to remember my father but I was told that my father was a good man and loved me as his own. I always wanted a father when I was growing up! And for some reason I always wanted to meet the person who murdered my Dad.

My mother's name was Irishstina Ann Jackson and for whatever reason, she always told people that she was from the "show me state" whenever she became upset. My mother was a good mother as a single mother of four (three girls, one boy). She did the best that she could to raise and to provide for us. I love my mother very much and I will always remember her as the number one mom in the world.

No Father or Mother to Offer Guidance

Unfortunately my mother was not strong enough to continue facing and standing up to all the problems that life put on her. She looked for and found her peace of mind in the use of drugs and alcohol. Tragically on June 1, 1990, at 6:30 PM that Friday evening my mother was pronounced dead.

The cause of my mother's death was a drug overdose. Sadly my mother was pregnant with twins when she died. My mother was 33 years old at the time of her death. She was so young and certainly too young to have died.

I was 14 years old when my mother died. I remember feeling like life doesn't matter to me anymore and as I had no father and now no mother, I felt like I wanted to die myself. I never had a male figure in my life to guide me positively to the duties of manhood. I never had a positive example to follow in my transformation from a boy to a man! I was a little boy in pain being emotionally destroyed by all that was happening to me in my life. I just wanted to feel loved and accepted by somebody. I wanted a family. I just wanted to feel like somebody. At 14 years old I felt like I had nobody to turn to. I felt like nobody understood me and how I was feeling about the loss of my mother. I turned to my childhood friends in my neighborhood because they are the only people that I felt understood me. For the most part we all were fatherless and had drug addicted mothers. Everyone called us trouble makers and told us that we all would be dead or in prison before our 18th birthdays (Sadly, these predictions were correct).

Wrong Choices

By this time in my life I didn't care about what people said about me or my childhood friends because the truth is that, I found love and acceptance in my friends—they were the only family that I had known. None of us had parents to tell us what to do or when to come in, or where to go to school etc. For the most part we all did whatever we wanted to do. We had no curfew so staying out on the streets until two or three o'clock in the morning was normal for us. As a child I had so much anger inside of me, I didn't care about who I hurt nor did I care about what might happen to me. I hated God. I hated life and honestly I hated being me. In 1991 shortly before my daughter was born, I committed a horrifying crime. I shot and killed a man in his own home. On June 9, 1992 (at 16 years old), I turned myself in to the Milwaukee police department for the crime I had committed. I was sent to a juvenile detention center and shortly thereafter I was waived and moved to the adult court system. (I never seen or hugged my daughter as a free man.)

My being 16 years old at the time, I didn't understand anything about the law nor the legal troubles that I was in. I was kept among adult repeat offenders and they repeatedly told me to go to jury trial and to not take the plea deal that my public defender attorney advised me to take. As I listened to these adults, I went to jury trial, (against my own choice) and I was found guilty of 1st degree intentional homicide.

On Jan. 5, 1993—three months before my 17th birthday—I was sentenced to life in prison with a parole eligibility date set for January, 2025.

Time to Think About the Seriousness of the Crime

At the time I committed my crime I didn't understand the seriousness of what I had done. I didn't understand the seriousness of what I had done to the victim or myself. It wasn't until I was around 29 years old, that I finally began to realize the true reality of what I had done. It was at this time that I began to realize and fully understand how much pain that I had caused my victim's family, and that I had taken a life from this world.

I then started thinking about the relationship between actions and consequences. This started me to thinking about good choices rather than fast bad choices. With this I began to adopt positive change in my life. I begin to think before acting. I started to understand the importance of making productive decisions rather than destructive decisions. I finally understand the power of positive thinking.

I have learned so much in prison. I understand that some mistakes I will never stop paying for and that I have to learn to live and deal with my life problems in a responsible manner. I have learned how to accept responsibility for all my actions. As a child I didn't know how to accept responsibility for my actions because I always made an excuse and put blame for my action on the things that I been through as a child.

Maturing and Hoping for a Second Chance

As my mind matured, I came to realize that I am the only person that is responsible for my actions, and for all the choices that I make in my life. As a man I accept full responsibility for everything I have done. I have made so many mistakes and I have learned from my mistakes but most importantly I have also learned from the mistakes of others.

As a mentally matured adult I don't believe that I should be let off the hook for my crimes as a juvenile. I believe that everyone should be punished for any and all criminal activity in which he or she involve themselves in whether he or she be a juvenile or an adult; however I strongly believe in second chances! I don't believe that a 15-year-old or a 16-year-old juvenile should be sent to prison for life as if a juvenile can't change his or her ways of thinking.

Juveniles can change and I believe that all juveniles should be given a second chance to prove that their destructive behavior could be transformed into positive constructive behavior if given the chance to prove it. I'm a 33-year-old man. I been in prison since I was 16 years old and since I been in prison I have changed my way of thinking and I have changed my behavioral patterns. I have earned my H.S.E.D. [High School Equivalency Diploma] and I became a licensed barber/cosmetologist. I have took classes on character development and I'm constantly trying to better myself as a person.

My goals are to be home with my 17-year-old daughter that would love for me to be a part of her life. If paroled I want to open my own barbershop and start an Intervention program for troubled teens to help them to not make the same mistakes that I have made.

I am praying for a second chance at real life.

> "Sentencing youth to life without parole
> strips our young people of hope and the
> opportunity for rehabilitation."

A Mother of a Murder Victim Argues That Minors Should Not Be Sentenced to Life Without Parole

Personal Narrative

Linda L. White

In the following viewpoint, the mother of a murder victim details how she came to terms with the brutal crime and the juvenile offenders who committed the act. The author argues that juvenile criminals should not be put away for good because, of all criminals, they have the greatest capacity to reform. After meeting with one of her daughter's murderers, she was moved by his remorse, convincing her that young criminals deserve a chance for parole. Linda L. White testified before the House of Representatives Judicial Committee in support of legislation that would bar life without parole sentencing for young people; however, the Juvenile Justice Accountability and Improvement Act of 2009 did not make it into law.

Linda L. White, Testimony, Hearing on "Juvenile Life Without Possibility of Parole," House Judicial Committee, June 9, 2009.

Mr. Chairman and members: Thank you for inviting me to discuss the issue of juvenile life without possibility of parole, and specifically H.R. 2289, the Juvenile Justice Accountability and Improvement Act of 2009. My name is Linda White and, as stated above, I am a member of Murder Victims' Families for Reconciliation. I live near Houston, Texas, where I have resided for 35 years. I am here to support the bill before you because it allows for periodic reviews of life without parole sentences given to juveniles.

Gaining Knowledge Through Tragic Circumstances

Until November of 1986, I was not very knowledgeable or very interested, to be quite frank, in criminal justice matters in general, and certainly not juvenile justice matters. That changed quite suddenly and dramatically late that November when our 26-year-old daughter Cathy went missing for five days and was then found dead following a sexual assault by two 15-year-old boys. I spent the better part of a year in limbo awaiting their trials, as they had both been certified to stand trial as adults.

During that time, the only information I had on either of them was that they both had long juvenile records. There was never any doubt about their guilt, as they had confessed to the rape and murder and lead the police to her body after they had been detained by the police in another city in Texas. The court-appointed attorneys for both pled them out and they were sentenced to long prison terms with no chance at parole for at least eighteen years. They came up for parole in 2004 and were both given five year set-offs [delays in parole review], so they remain in prison at this time. I assume they will come up again later on this year.

A Newfound Belief in Restorative Justice

The year after my daughter was murdered, I returned to college to become a death educator and grief counselor. Since that time,

I have received a bachelor's degree in psychology, a master's degree in clinical psychology, and a doctorate in educational human resource development with a focus in adult education. I fell in love with teaching along the way and never got my professional counseling credentials, but I have counseled informally through church and my teaching. During the time I taught at the university level, I taught upper level college courses for eight and a half years in prison, the most rewarding work I have ever done, and the most healing for me as the mother of a murder victim.

In addition to the formal schooling I've had, I have also educated myself in the area of criminal justice. I heard a lot of information when I attended victims' groups and I wanted to know if it was accurate. I have found out that, for the most part, it was not. One notable example: Texas prisons are about as far as you can get from country clubs. Many of our citizens, and certainly victims of crime, want the men and women who are convicted of criminal activity to suffer as much as possible in prison, believing that this is the way they will turn from a life of crime. I no longer believe this to be true, and I have become a devout believer in restorative justice as opposed to retributive justice. It does not mean that I think incarceration is always wrong, but neither do I believe that it should be our first inclination, for juveniles or for adults. And neither am I a great believer in long sentences, for most offenders. As a psychology student and teacher, I have learned that punishment is the least effective means to change behavior, and that it often has negative side effects as well.

Facing the Young Murderers

My journey to healing after my daughter's murder was different than what I often see in victim/survivors, for I had concentrated on healing for my family and me, and because I focused on education over the years. At first it was education about grief and how to help my young granddaughter with hers, and then, when I returned to college, it became about psychology and issues related to death and dying. Eventually, it became concen-

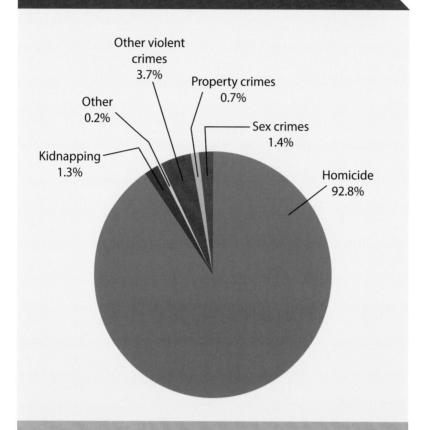

CRIMES COMMITTED BY YOUTH SENTENCED TO LIFE WITHOUT PAROLE IN THE UNITED STATES

Other violent crimes
3.7%

Property crimes
0.7%

Other
0.2%

Sex crimes
1.4%

Kidnapping
1.3%

Homicide
92.8%

Taken from: Amnesty International and Human Rights Watch, "The Rest of Their Lives: Life Without Parole for Child Offenders in the United States," October 11, 2005.

trated in criminal justice. Early on I saw much that was violent in our system—perhaps necessarily so at times—but still, it seemed to me that we returned violence for violence in so many ways. I kept my mind and heart open to another means of doing justice, one that would be based on non-violent ideals and means. Restorative justice is that paradigm and I have become one of its greatest proponents. That is what actually led me to seek a mediated conversation with either of the young men who killed my Cathy.

As I said previously, for many years, I only knew that the boys who killed my daughter were juveniles with long criminal records. In 2000, I found out that one of them, Gary Brown, was willing to meet with me in a mediated dialogue as part of a program that we have in our Texas Department of Criminal Justice's Victims' Services Division. He was apparently very remorseful by that time and had prayed for a chance to tell us that. During the next year, Gary, with the help of our mediator Ellen Halbert, and my daughter Ami (Cathy's daughter whom we had raised and adopted) and I did a great deal of reflective work to prepare for our meeting. During that time I found out from Gary's records that his long juvenile record began at the age of eight with his running away from abusive situations, both at home and in foster care eventually. If I were being abused emotionally, physically, and sexually, I think I'd run away, too; it seems quite rational to me. I also found out that his first suicide attempt was at the age of eight, the first of ten attempts. I have a grandson just about that age right now, and it breaks my heart to think of a child like that trying to take his own life because it is so miserable.

Until the time that I met with Gary, I had never laid eyes on him and had, over the years, gradually come to ignore his existence. Both the offenders became non-persons to me, in effect. Once I knew that Gary wanted to meet me, that non-personhood totally changed for me; he became as human to me as the men I had taught in prison. That in and of itself was a relief, I think, since part of me revolted at the idea of forgetting him in any way at all. As the time approached for us to meet, I know that my daughter and Gary both became more and more apprehensive, but not me. I couldn't wait to see him and tell him how much I believed in his remorse and was grateful for it. I know that this unusual response to the killer of one's beloved child was only possible through my discovery of restorative justice and, of course, by the grace of God. I strongly believe that most of my journey over the last 22 years had been through grace. Otherwise, I have no explanation for it.

Juvenile Offenders Should Have the Opportunity to Reform

My meeting with him was everything I expected and more. Since it was made into a documentary [*Meeting with a Killer*], I have been privileged to have it shown around the world for training and educational purposes, and I have heard from many who have seen it and felt blessed by the experience. I am sometimes invited to go with the film to answer questions and reflect on my experience. I also go into prison, especially with a victim/offender encounter program we have in Texas called Bridges to Life, a faith-based restorative justice curriculum, where my film is used to educate offenders related to victim empathy. I have been deeply blessed by this work and I feel Cathy's presence in it every time I stand before a group either in or out of prison and reflect on my journey.

My education and years of teaching developmental psychology have taught me that young people are just different qualitatively from the adults we hope they become. And my experience with Gary has taught me that we have a responsibility to protect our youth from the kind of childhood that he had, and from treatment that recklessly disregards their inherent vulnerability as children. Sentencing youth to life without parole strips our young people of hope and the opportunity for rehabilitation. It ignores what science tells us: that youth are fundamentally different from adults both physically and emotionally. Even given the trauma, and incredible loss my family experienced, I still believe that young people need to be held accountable in a way that reflects their ability to grow and change. Gary is proof that young people, even those who have done horrible things, can be reformed.

> "*The sentence of life without parole
> assured us that the killer would never
> enjoy the freedoms of a life he had so
> brutally taken from another.*"

The Sister of a Murder Victim Urges Legislators Not to Abolish the Life Without Parole Sentence for Juvenile Murderers

Personal Narrative

Bobbi Jamriska

In the following viewpoint, the sister of a murder victim addresses the Pennsylvania Senate regarding juvenile sentencing laws permitting life without parole for minors. The author argues that her sister's killer deserved his life without parole sentence because of the brutality of his crime. She contends that such individuals belong behind bars so that other families will not risk having these killers strike again. Bobbi Jamriska is the vice president of the National Organization of Victims of Juvenile Lifers.

First, I'd like to thank the committee members for holding hearings on what I consider a public safety issue and informing and involving victims' families in the process. I am absolutely opposed to any changes that will result in future sentencing laws or any changes that will allow previously sentenced offenders to new hearings or possible parole.

A Brutal Murder and an Unfeeling Killer

In order to express why my feelings on the subject are so strong, I'd like to start by telling you about my little sister. My sister, Kristina Grill, was 15 years old when she was brutally murdered by another 15 year old. The murderer was her ex boyfriend, and quite possibly the person she loved and trusted most in this world. You see, Kristina was approximately 5 months pregnant on the day she left this world at the hands of her killer. In a violent rage over my sister's intentions to keep her unborn child and tell my mother and step-father about her pregnancy, Inmate #CS9937 brutally murdered her. The details of the crime are that a 15-year-old pregnant teenage girl was stabbed 11 times about the neck, and punched and kicked repeatedly. Her killer had brought a kitchen knife to the meeting place they had mutually agreed upon. The pictures of her bruised and beaten face shown at the trial are the stuff of my nightmares and sleepless nights to this very day. The police were able to identify shoe prints on her belly where the baby was growing inside her, as well as on her face and legs. As her killer watched her bleed to death in the school yard, he later described her body as 'twitching' as he zipped up her jacket to ebb the flow of blood from her neck. He then, left her in an elementary school yard to die, hid the murder weapon on his way home, hid his bloody clothes in his house, showered and went about his day. Fortunately for us, if anything in this story can be construed as fortunate, my sister, Kristina, had kept an extensive diary, the last entry reading, ". . . Reese came down my house, he said we need to talk so he said meet him at 2:00

tomorrow at Elliot Park he better be there." Those last, haunting words in a teenage girl's diary are the lead the police needed to find and eventually convict a brutal murderer.

An Event That Touches Everyone

There is no way in human words or expression that anyone will ever be able to convey the grief and pain that the survivors of a victim of violent crime such as this experience. The normal human experience of death and loss, whether sudden or expected, is one most people can say they have experienced. The added pain and suffering of knowing that another human being brought about your loved one's end is immeasurable. In time, you learn to live with the pain. It never goes away, it's always right there below the surface of your every moment of life. The years pass, and along with it come milestones or anniversaries that will never occur. In Krissy's case, I recently contemplated what would have been her 30th birthday, not to mention the observation that my niece or nephew who died that day would just now be starting high school. Everyone around you goes on living, loving, and enjoying life, but that piece of you is gone forever and shadows everything that comes after that moment. That pain, and those moments suffered by survivors are something that cannot be represented on a graph or a chart of statistics. However, it is quite important that when one considers the implications of changing sentencing laws or parole guidelines that pain be weighed.

We went to trial a week after my Mother died, 9 months after Krissy's murder. My mother, you see, could not bear the pain I alluded to in the last paragraph and just gave up on living. At the trial, after the evidence of the crime and its cruelty were presented, the defendant had his turn to speak. His defense centered on his poor upbringing and abusive family. The jury was smart enough to see that despite those conditions, a brutal, cold blooded 15-year-old killer needed to be incarcerated for life. Both for the crime he committed, and to insure he could never inflict that kind of pain on any other victims or families. At the end of the judicial phase, we as a family tried to get on with living and grieving. The justice system had given us the justice it could to help us come to terms with all that had transpired. The sentence of life without parole assured us that the killer would never enjoy the freedoms of a life he had so brutally taken from another.

Forcing Families to Relive the Pain

On August 22nd, 2008, I opened my mailbox to a letter from the Office of the Victim Advocate. As I opened the letter, the feeling was the psychological equivalent of ripping open an almost healed wound on the human body. Every last painful feeling, memory, and fear of that time came racing back. As I continued to absorb the impact that just holding these hearings would have on my coping with the loss, I grew angrier with each passing breath. You see, the justice system had offered me the best it had in the face of insurmountable tragedy, life without parole. How could there be a way this could possibly be revisited, and furthermore, how could that be done in the name of humanity? Where was the humanity in my pregnant sister bleeding to death in an elementary school yard?

I have made it a point in the past few weeks to read up on this subject as much as possible in preparation for these hearings. One thing that is obvious is that the victim's voice is not one clearly heard on this subject. I would like to make it clear that is not for lack of concern with the issue, it is more likely tied to the emotional pain and upheaval fighting this fight will bring the families.

The Human Rights Watch [HRW] is entrenched in a nationwide battle to effect change in the mandatory sentencing of juveniles, and recommends [in its 2005 report *The Rest of Their Lives*] that legislators:

> Enact legislation that abolishes the sentence of life without parole for any offense committed by a child. Such legislation

should include a retroactivity provision enabling current child offenders serving life without parole to have their cases reviewed by a court for re-assessment and re-sentencing to a sentence with the possibility of parole.

In doing so, you will subject, in the state of Pennsylvania, over three hundred families to the pain of reliving the murder and death of their loved ones all over again. The HRW would have you believe that a parole hearing and consideration for inmates would be a fair and humane answer to the problem. As a victim's family member, the pain that one parole hearing, let alone multiple hearings over many years, would cause is inconceivable. There is no semblance of humanity in inflicting that kind of pain on families who have already lost and suffered so much.

Dismissing Arguments for Changes in Parole Laws

In its studies, HRW identifies four reasons leading to bad decisions made by juvenile offenders facing criminal charges that can lead to life in prison; they include: waiving their rights, taking bad advice from attorneys, low levels of education, and not understanding the consequences. To each of those four issues faced by murderers and co-conspirators in murder I would answer, there is still a dead human being on the other end of the issue. The actor's level of education or law advice does NOT change the fact that a family somewhere has buried a loved one prematurely for that convicted criminal's actions.

Another prominent argument for re-evaluating juvenile sentences is that the sentencing often takes place for offenders who have never committed another crime. The previously non-violent offender who murdered my sister had never been in trouble with the law. That fact has no bearing on the brutality or lack of humanity it took to carry out his actions. The past record of an offender at any age, who takes a life in a manner that is tried as an adult, is really a non factor to the act itself. There is still a dead human being who cannot speak for themselves at the base of the issue.

Pennsylvania Should Not Focus Its Reform Laws on Murderers

These are not the individuals we should take a chance on and hope they have been rehabilitated and allow them to walk the streets, live in our neighborhoods, and see our children. This committee has done an outstanding job of trying to address the prison population increase and improve diversionary programs by focusing on less violent offenders. That is the cohort group our collective attention should be focused on—not on letting out murderers early.

Pennsylvania District Attorneys Association, Testimony Before the State House of Representatives Judiciary Committee on HB1999, August 4, 2010.

In Pennsylvania, the intention of these hearings and the desire of the parties seeking them are to review cases where offenders were secondary to the crime. A passenger in a car is sentenced to life when someone else does the killing, for example. The problem is that you cannot just selectively undo the law without overarching ramifications. To make the changes to the law being considered also means that human beings capable of kicking and stabbing a pregnant young girl to death will also get the opportunity to be freed. As lawmakers and members of the community, it is the responsibility of everyone on this panel to ensure that never happens for the safety of the community at large.

Focus on Prevention

The question in my mind is, if the juvenile life sentence rate in Pennsylvania is so much higher than that of comparably populated states, what are those states doing differently for their children? The resolution of the high crime and conviction rates among teens is NOT to change the law so fewer children are sentenced. The resolution of the issue is through a thorough understanding of what creates child murderers and implement change to social and or economic factors that drive that behavior. It would be of great benefit for this committee to explore the successes of states like New Jersey who do not have this issue, find out what they do differently for their teens, and then use State resources to effect change. To use a legislative mandate to lower the number of juveniles serving life sentences as a solution is equivalent to placing 10,000 more motorcycles on the road to make motorcycle safety statistics improve. In both cases, the problem still exists as it did before; it just looks better on a graph or statistical report.

In closing, I would ask that you each think about the damage and pain such a review would cause families who have already lost and suffered more than anyone can comprehend. I know that inmate #CS9937 is currently being housed in a correctional facility 15 minutes from his family. I also know that my sister is buried in a cemetery 15 minutes from my house. We both have the opportunity to visit our loved ones when we wish. The one difference is that I can never hear her speak or see her face again. The only thing that makes that bearable as a victim is the knowledge that the monster who committed my sister to her grave will also never experience the life he took away from her. The number of juveniles serving these sentences in Pennsylvania is alarming, but this is not the path needed to solve the issue.

Organizations to Contact

The editors have compiled the following list of organizations concerned with the issues debated in this book. The descriptions are derived from materials provided by the organizations. All have publications or information available for interested readers. The list was compiled on the date of publication of the present volume; the information provided here may change. Be aware that many organizations take several weeks or longer to respond to inquiries, so allow as much time as possible.

American Civil Liberties Union (ACLU)
125 Broad Street, 18th Floor
New York, NY 10004
(212) 549-2500
website: www.aclu.org

The ACLU works to ensure that the rights of all Americans are observed and protected, with a special emphasis on groups who have historically experienced discrimination and a lack of rights. Its focus ranges from capital punishment and free speech to racial justice and women's rights. With regard to juvenile justice, the ACLU believes that the criminal justice system in the United States must be reformed so that the punishment of a minor leads to rehabilitation and productive adult citizens. Publications such as "End Juvenile Life in Prison without Parole," "From Filthy Boys Prison to New Beginning: Hill Staffers Walk a Mile in Youthful Offenders' Shoes," and "Lift Children Out of the Criminal Justice System—Don't Lock Them Away," can be found on the organization's website.

American Psychological Association (APA)
750 First Street, NE
Washington, DC 20002-4242

(800) 374-2721, (202) 336-5500
website: www.apa.org

The APA is the largest scientific and professional organization of psychologists. With regard to juvenile justice reform, the APA believes that the juvenile justice system should focus on the unique mental states of at-risk youth and emphasize rehabilitation instead of incarceration. Articles exploring the mental health of juvenile offenders and rehabilitation programs can be found on the APA website.

Amnesty International

5 Penn Plaza, 16th Floor
New York, NY 10001
(212) 807-8400 • fax: (212) 463-9193
e-mail: admin-us@aiusa.org
website: www.amnesty.org

Amnesty International is a global human rights organization that seeks to promote and protect the basic rights of all individuals worldwide. Abolishing the death penalty, detention and imprisonment issues, and discrimination fall among the many campaigns the organization has coordinated. It opposes the death penalty for children and has fought to see the sentences of incarcerated youths shortened. Detailed publications about specific cases such as "USA: Child Sentenced to Life Seeks Clemency: Jacqueline Montanez," and more general articles such as "USA Must Halt Life Without Parole Sentences for Children" are available on the organization's website.

Campaign for Youth Justice (CFYJ)

1012 14th Street NW, Suite 610
Washington, DC 20005
(202) 558-3580 • fax (202) 386-9807
e-mail: info@cfyj.org
website: www.campaignforyouthjustice.org

CFYJ is working to stop the incarceration of youth under eighteen in adult courts. In partnership with state-based campaigns, the organization provides a wide range of information about the problems associated with trying youths as adults and works to empower individuals who have been most harmed by the current system. The organization's website provides resources to help parents whose children have been tried or incarcerated as well as those who feel the need to speak out against the current system.

Center for Juvenile Justice Reform
Georgetown University
PO Box 571444
3300 Whitehaven Street NW, Suite 5000
Washington, DC 200057-1485
(202) 687-7657 • fax (202) 687-3110
website: cjjr.georgetown.edu

The Center for Juvenile Justice Reform promotes the adoption of a juvenile justice system that seeks to reduce delinquency through the implementation of a balanced, multi-system approach that encourages both development and accountability. One of the main focuses of the program is "crossover youth" or those individuals who are part of both the child welfare and juvenile justice systems. Detailed information about the Crossover Youth Practice Model, the Juvenile Justice System Improvement Project, the Breakthrough Series Collaborative, and Models for Change can be found on the center's website.

Coalition for Juvenile Justice (CJJ)
1319 F Street NW, Suite 402
Washington, DC 20004
(202) 467-0864 • fax (202) 887-0738
e-mail: info@juvjustice.org
website: www.juvjustice.org

CJJ serves as a central organizing body for state advisory groups and allies who work to reduce the number of juvenile offenders. Through its publications, conferences, and leadership, the organization works to educate the public and advise policy makers on federal juvenile justice issues. Fact sheets, position papers, newsletters, and reports can be found on the CJJ website.

Human Rights Watch (HRW)

350 Fifth Avenue, 34th Floor
New York, NY 10118-3299
(212) 290-4700
website: www.hrw.org

HRW fights to ensure that the human rights of individuals around the world are upheld. The organization's work spans a wide range of topics from arms and counterterrorism to business and the environment. The rights of juvenile offenders within the criminal justice system have been an ongoing focus for the organization. HRW has urged the United States to end the life without parole sentence for juvenile offenders and consider the hardships that youths face when incarcerated in adult prisons. The HRW website provides additional information about these topics and others relating to juvenile justice.

National Center for Juvenile Justice (NCJJ)

3700 South Water Street, Suite 200
Pittsburgh, PA 15203
(412) 227-6950 • fax (412) 227-6955
e-mail: ncjj@ncjfcj.org
website: www.ncjj.org

NCJJ has served as the research arm of the National Council of Juvenile and Family Court Judges since 1973. Its mission is to conduct independent and original research on juvenile justice topics. NCJJ's extensive research database includes national and state profiles of the juvenile justice system as well as publications on a range of issues including child welfare, intervention services, and recidivism.

National Center for Mental Health and Juvenile Justice (NCMHJJ)

345 Delaware Avenue
Delmar, NY 12054
(866) 962-6455 • fax (518) 439-7612
e-mail: ncmhjj@prainc.com
website: www.ncmhjj.com

NCMHJJ was formed in 2001 to tackle the mental health needs of minors going through the juvenile justice system. Models for Change is one initiative through which the organization hopes to create change within the juvenile justice system. The NCMHJJ website provides information about the ongoing activities of this project and others as well as a database of publications concerning the juvenile justice system and mental health.

Office of Juvenile Justice and Delinquency Prevention (OJJDP)

810 Seventh Street NW
Washington, DC 20531
(202) 307-5911
website: www.ojjdp.gov

Part of the US Department of Justice, OJJDP is the US government agency charged by Congress to face the challenge of juvenile offenders and propose new policies to help solve this problem. The office works closely with state, local, and tribal jurisdictions to assist in the implementation of juvenile justice solutions. Some of the programs run by the OJJDP include Disproportionate Minority Contact, Girls Study Group, and the Juvenile Accountability Block Grants Program—each designed to focus on a specific area of the juvenile justice system. More details about these programs along with publications regarding juvenile justice are available on the OJJDP website.

Prison Policy Initiative (PPI)
PO Box 127
Northampton, MA 01061
website: www.prisonpolicy.org

PPI is a non-profit organization dedicated to publicizing the effects of mass incarceration on individuals, communities, and national welfare with the hope that the public will use this information to improve the criminal justice system. Information about youth correctional facilities in various states and reports on the effects of incarceration on juvenile offenders can be accessed on the PPI website.

Sentencing Project
1705 DeSales Street NW
Washington, DC 20036
(202) 628-0871fax (202) 628-1091
e-mail: staff@sentencingproject.org
website: www.sentencingproject.org

The Sentencing Project was founded in 1986 with the goal of reforming the US criminal justice system. To achieve this goal the organization has sought changes in sentencing policy, the end of discriminatory practices, and alternative punishments to incarceration. The Sentencing Project advocates a reshaping of the juvenile justice system that emphasizes rehabilitation over harsh punishment. Extensive information about the Sentencing Project's views on this issue can be read on the organization's website.

Southern Poverty Law Center (SPLC)
400 Washington Avenue
Montgomery, AL 36104
(334) 956-8200
website: www.splcenter.org

SPLC is an organization that advocates for underrepresented populations' civil rights. It educates the public about civil rights issues and prosecutes cases that highlight these rights within the justice system. One issue of particular emphasis for the SPLC is children at risk within underrepresented communities, particularly African American and Latino children. SPLC works to ensure that these children's juvenile justice rights are observed when they do encounter the system and seeks to reform the system so that it gives these children the opportunity to become contributing members of society. Detailed reports on issues relating to at-risk children can be read on the organization's website.

For Further Reading

Books

John Aarons, Lisa Smith, and Linda Wagner, *Dispatches from Juvenile Hall: Fixing a Failing System*. New York: Penguin, 2009.

Thomas J. Barnard and Megan C. Kurlychek, *The Cycle of Juvenile Justice*. New York: Oxford University Press, 2010.

David Chura, *I Don't Wish Nobody to Have a Life Like Mine: Tales of Kids in Adult Lockup*. Boston: Beacon, 2010.

Jeffrey Fagan and Franklin E. Zimring, *The Changing Borders of Juvenile Justice: Transfer of Adolescents to the Criminal Court*. Chicago: University of Chicago Press, 2000.

Thomas Grisso and Robert G. Schwartz, *Youth on Trial: A Developmental Perspective on Juvenile Justice*. Chicago: University of Chicago Press, 2003.

Edward Humes, *No Matter How Loud I Shout: A Year in the Life of Juvenile Court*. New York: Touchstone, 1996.

Barry Krisberg, *Juvenile Justice: Redeeming Our Children*. Thousand Oaks, CA: Sage, 2005.

Aaron Kupchik, *Judging Juveniles: Prosecuting Adolescents in Adult and Juvenile Courts*. New York: New York University Press, 2006.

Steve Liss, *No Place for Children: Voices from Juvenile Detention*. Austin: University of Texas Press, 2005.

Anne M. Nurse, *Locked Up, Locked Out: Young Men in the Juvenile Justice System*. Nashville: Vanderbilt University Press, 2010.

Adam D. Reich, *Hidden Truth: Young Men Navigating Lives in and out of Juvenile Prison*. Berkeley: University of California Press, 2010.

Mark Salzman, *True Notebooks: A Writer's Year at Juvenile Hall*. New York: Vintage, 2004.

Elizabeth S. Scott and Laurence Steinberg, *Rethinking Juvenile Justice*. Cambridge, MA: Harvard University Press, 2008.

Randall G. Shelden, *Delinquency and Juvenile Justice in American Society*. Long Grove, IL: Waveland, 2012.

Randall G. Shelden and Daniel Macallair, *Juvenile Justice in America: Problems and Prospects*. Long Grove, IL: Waveland, 2007.

Christopher Slobogin and Mark R. Fondacaro, *Juveniles at Risk: A Plea for Preventive Justice*. New York: Oxford University Press, 2011.

Irene Sullivan, *Raised by the Courts: One Judge's Insight into Juvenile Justice*. New York: Kaplan, 2010.

David S. Tanenhaus, *Juvenile Justice in the Making*. New York: Oxford University Press, 2005.

Periodicals and Internet Sources

Neelum Arya, "State Trends: Legislative Changes from 2005 to 2010 Removing Youth from the Adult Criminal Justice System," Campaign for Youth Justice, 2011. www.campaign foryouthjustice.org.

Pete Brook, "Uncompromising Photos Expose Juvenile Detention in America," *Wired*, April 11, 2012. www.wired.com.

Karen Brown, "Positive Youth Development," *Child Law Practice*, March 2010.

Caitlin Flanagan, "The High Cost of Coddling," *Wall Street Journal*, April 17, 2009.

Gail Garinger, "Juveniles Don't Deserve Life Sentences," *New York Times,* March 15, 2012.

New York Times, "Locking Up Fewer Children," August 14, 2009.

Monica Potts, "Closed Circuit," *American Prospect,* January–February 2011.

Charles Puzzanchera and Benjamin Adams, "Juvenile Arrests 2009," *Juvenile Offenders and Victims: National Report Series Bulletin*, December 2011. www.ojjdp.gov.

Luis Rodríguez, "Juvenile Injustice," *Progressive,* July 2008.

Paula Schaefer, "Girls in the Juvenile Justice System," *GPSolo*, April–May 2008.

Irene Sullivan, "Keeping Kids Outside the System," *Reason,* July 2011.

Heather Anne Thompson, "Criminalizing Kids: The Overlooked Reason for Failing Schools," *Dissent,* Fall 2011.

Index